POEMS

STEFAN GEORGE

POEMS

Rendered into English by

CAROL NORTH VALHOPE AND ERNST MORWITZ

SCHOCKEN BOOKS · NEW YORK

CONTENTS

CONTENTS

Ernst Morwitz

STEFAN GEORGE

G REAT POETRY is not begotten behind sheltering walls. Its growth is intertwined with the life of individuals and of groups, with the rise and fall in the destiny of peoples. So it is not surprising that great poems always originate at turns of the tide in the affairs of men, when an old era is dying out and a new era is tuning its first song. That is the moment for the poet to 'charm the air to give a sound.' Homer and the Greek tragedians lived in periods when the fate of the Greeks trembled in the balance. Dante wrote at the turn of Italian, Shakespeare at that of English history. Goethe's work marks the beginning of national unity for which he created the necessary unified and unifying language. When Germany had reached the peak of external power and her inner strength began to lessen, another true poet at the turn of her destiny comprised the present and the future: Stefan George. In an age when everything was flattened to the same level, when rattling of sabers and playing with sugary words were both manifestations of the same impulse to hide inner emptiness under the guise of being 'interesting,' this man was the only one whose life and work were governed by the same stern law. He was the last of a series of relentless thinkers and of those great poets who blended profundity with enchantment. He not only produced poems of enduring beauty and altered the tone and the structure of his language, he became the judge and the prophet of his people. And so he rings in a new era.

That poets direct the trends of their day, is frequently not

9

apparent during their life-time, but Stefan George's power was felt even thirty years before he died. When the First World War was still in the offing, the best of Germany's younger generation tried to shape the pattern of their lives to the ideas they had derived from his poems. When the war had come, soldiers carried his books in their packs along with Goethe's Faust, and after it was over, his influence grew from year to year. His younger friends, schooled in his thought, held important positions in almost all of the leading German universities, and members of the youth movements that were gaining in scope and importance, declaimed his poems at their reunions. In view of this, it is understandable that the rising Nazi government, intent upon capturing youth for its aims and purposes, tried to enlist his services for its cause. In 1933 he was offered the presidency of the Academy for Literature with an annual endowment, either to be retained by him or to be awarded as he wished. In addition to this, he was asked to choose any other official position he might fancy. He refused this offer in all its tempting ramifications. He did not even answer it himself, but asked the author of this introduction to communicate his decision to the government, to emphasize his wish to preserve his complete independence: he did not wish to be the president of an Academy since he had never believed in such institutions; he did not wish to receive money either as an honorary remuneration for himself, or as a grant for others, and he did not wish to discuss the boundaries between art and politics with members of the government. Then, as an unambiguous protest against totalitarian compulsion and the increasing misinterpretation and misapplication of his ideas and his words, he left his country and spent the rest of his life as a voluntary exile in Switzerland, in the same moderate circumstances as before.

STEFAN GEORGE was born on July 12, 1868, in the village of Buedesheim near Bingen. On his father's side he came of peasant stock that for hundreds of years had lived in Upper Lorraine, a region that blended French and German characteristics. His mother's family had been landed proprietors on the Rhine for many generations. He spent his childhood in Bingen where his father moved in 1878 to carry on the wine trade. This little city is weighed with historical memories, and unites the traces of various civilizations: a Roman bridge and the ruins of Roman strongholds, stones from unknown periods in the history of the Germanic tribes and Romanesque and Gothic churches of the Middle Ages where incense still mingled with the prayers of suppliants, in George's lifetime, as it did centuries ago. Vineyards that yield the famous Rhine wines frame the city, and here the river turns northward in a green tide between narrowing shores of rock.

Even as a child, Stefan George evinced a deep interest in the sound and structure of language and literature. At the age of nine, he invented a new secret language far richer in vowels than his native tongue. Vestiges of this are preserved in the closing lines of his poem 'Origins' (p. 159) in which he glorifies the forces that fed the dreams of his childhood: the Romans who had brought civilization to the wilderness of Western Germany. The Church utilized the latent Roman trends for its teachings of the Hereafter. Romanesque architecture still upheld the connection between body and earth; the Gothic symbolizes the straining of the soul away from the caging flesh. But even in early youth, the poet felt that the heritage of antiquity, the joy in the things of this earth, had never entirely vanished from his native land, and he sings this joy, not in words but in sounds that convey only the emotional quality.

In the autumn of 1881, he entered the Gymnasium in Darmstadt where he became proficient in Greek and Latin and continued his courses in English, Italian and French. On completing his schooling (1888), he decided to devote himself to the study of modern languages. London was his first destination and here he became familiar with a more liberal and individualistic form of life than his own country was able to afford him at that time. But he made no friends, and later he visited England only once, to see Ernest Dowson, whose poems had aroused the admiration of Albert Verwey. The poet Verwey, the painter Jan Toorop, and the architect Berlage were George's Dutch friends.

To continue his studies in French, he went to Montreux in French Switzerland, and then, after a first brief visit to Northern Italy, proceeded to Paris. Almost immediately upon his arrival, in a Pension in the Rue de l'Abbé de l'Epée, he met the poet Albert Saint-Paul who made him acquainted with the writers and poets of the day. Soon he was admitted to the famous Tuesday evenings of Mallarmé whose small lodgings in the Rue de Rome limited the number of guests to twelve. Mallarmé, who introduced him to Verlaine, once said of him: 'Let this second Werther come to see me, but see that he leaves his pistol behind.'

It was at this time that he began his translation of Baudelaire, whom the French symbolists honored as their spiritual forebear. When in the autumn of 1892 the periodical 'La Plume' published a request for contributions to a Baudelaire memorial, George's signature appeared as that of the only German among those writers and poets, who, like him, had made Paris their intellectual focus: Leconte de Lisle, Paul Bourget, François Coppée, Achille Delaroche, Anatole France, Edmond de Goncourt, Hérédia, Huysmans, Lemonnier, Mallarmé, Mirbeau,

Jean Moréas, de Régnier, Richepin, Rodenbach, Waclav Rolicz-Lieder, Paul Verlaine, Francis Vielé-Griffin and Stuart Merrill.

After a journey to Northern and Central Spain which he considered of the utmost significance for his inner development, he went to Berlin to attend lectures on linguistics and literature. He was repelled by contemporary German verse, which he regarded as a feeble imitation of classical and romantic poetry. His condemnation of the naturalistic trend in the German literature of that decade was outspoken, for he believed that a work of art should be something other, something more than a banal reproduction of unimportant realities. Every locution of his contemporaries seemed stale to him, and he was forced to realize that before he could express his ideas and emotions, he would first have to create an adequate form of expression. In his profound distaste for the unfavorable conditions in his own country, he even planned to emigrate to Mexico with some young Mexicans whom he had known in Paris and had met again in Berlin where he spoke only Spanish during the early part of the year 1889, because he utterly lacked German companions.

In the meantime he continued his experiments in poetry with renewed vigor, but it was not until he had received recognition that he published some of these early poems in a book called his 'Primer.' This contains several poems drafted in a language invented by the poet, not the sound sequence of his childhood, a fragment of which is preserved in 'Origins,' but a highly developed language that is very similar to Spanish. Later these poems were worked over into German. The 'Primer' comprises the years 1886-1889. 'Prince Indra,' a poem written prior to 1886, is contained in the concluding volume of the complete edition of George's works. The first poems that met his own demands he published in 1890 under the title of 'Hymns.'

Denmark and frequently Italy were the goals of his journeys during the years that followed, but most of his time was spent in Paris among his former friends, and in Vienna, where he tried to establish a friendship with the young Austrian, Hugo von Hofmannsthal, who had just published his first poems. Associated with him and with the Belgian Paul Gérardy, he founded a journal, the first issue of which appeared in October 1892. The 'Blaetter fuer die Kunst,' published at irregular intervals and only for subscribers, through 1919, was so utterly different in form, language and content from anything of the kind known up to then, that the public neither understood it nor guessed that twelve yearly issues would actually appear. A very few people, among them the plain Mr. Cynamon who owned the obscure printing press in the slums of Berlin where George himself helped set up the first issues, predicted that this journal would color the whole future course of German literature and life. Today every writer, journalist and reporter writing in German, whether or not he wants to, whether or not he knows it, uses expressions coined by George, uses words quickened by him. In Germany, only Goethe and Heine before him had so sweeping and direct an influence that penetrated to the very minutiae of everyday life. The 'Blaetter fuer die Kunst' are now one of the rarities on the literary market and on the shelves of only a few libraries in the world.

During this period of his life, George visited his parents in Bingen for a part of every year and lived in Berlin and Munich the rest of the time. The midsummer months he spent in Switzerland. Italy he revisited rarely and not at all after 1913. On the occasion of his last visit there, he saw Greek architecture in Paestum, for the first and only time. During his last stay in Paris (1908) he met Auguste Rodin. The conversation between the two is recorded by the author of this introduction who was present at that meeting, in the last volume of the 'Blaetter fuer die Kunst.' André Gide, who saw George at that time, gives a description of him:

'Admirable tête de St. G. que depuis longtemps je souhaitais connaître et dont j'admire l'oeuvre, chaque fois que je parviens à la comprendre. Teint blanc bleuâtre, peau mate et plus tirée que ridée, belle accusation de l'ossature; impeccablement rasé, abondante et solide crinière, plus noire encore que grise et rejetée d'un coup en arrière. Mains de convalescent, très fines, exsangues, très expressives. Il parle peu, mais d'une voix profonde et qui force l'attention. Grande veste-redingote de clergyman avec deux agrafes dans le haut, qui s'ouvre sur une cravatte-écharpe de velours noir, passée par-dessus le col, et débordant. La simple glissière d'or d'un cordon qui retient montre ou monocle met un éclat discret dans tout ce noir . . .

'Il s'exprime dans notre langue sans faute aucune, encore qu'un peu craintivement, semble-t-il, et fait preuve d'une connaissance et compréhension surprenantes de nos auteurs, poètes en particulier; tout ceci sans fatuité, mais avec une conscience évidente de son évidente supériorité.' * (*André Gide, Oeuvres complètes, V. 403.*)

* '. . . Struck by the admirable head of St. G. whom I had long hoped to know and whose work I admire every time I manage to understand it. Complexion bluish-white, skin pale and more drawn than wrinkled, beautiful bone structure; impeccably shaved, compact and abundant mane, still more black than gray and thrown back in a solid mass. A convalescent's hands, very slender, bloodless, very expressive. He talks little, but in a deep voice that demands attention. Large clergyman's frock coat with two clasps at the top,

George was always proud of never having a permanent home, of not depending upon worldly possessions and of leading a wandering life with only one aim: the search for men to share his views and his form of being. In his detailed history of the 'Blaetter fuer die Kunst,' Friedrich Wolters cites some of those who played an important role in George's life. George himself dedicated poems to them, but beyond this, and without mention of names, human beings are the very stuff of which his poems are made. For he, who had the reputation of being haughty and inaccessible and who shunned publicity, loved the contact with people of all levels and liked to emphasize that a workingman often understood him better than an intellectual. Every line of his works reflects people and experiences that were important to him. In this sense his writing constitutes a complete diary, and thus the following summary of his works automatically gives the outline of his inner biography.

In the 'Hymns' (Berlin, 1890) the contours of the new language he had striven for are definitely drawn. It is more stern and sparing and richer in vowel sounds than the language of poetry prior to George. Relative clauses are used only where it is inevitable. Emotions are not described or analyzed, but communicated by impressions made on the ear and eye. The imagery frequently seems obscure through its compression. These poems, in this language, have nothing in common with the hymns of the Christian Church; rather do they derive from

---

opening on a black velvet stock tied on top of the collar and flowing over it. The simple gold slide-ring of a cord that holds watch or monocle introduces a discreet brilliance into all this black . . .

'He expresses himself faultlessly in our language, although a bit timidly, it seems, and shows an astonishing knowledge and comprehension of our authors, poets in particular; all this without conceit but with an obvious consciousness of his obvious superiority.'

Pindar's hymns, where an ecstasy of rhythm and the magic of sound lift actual experience to the heights of poetry. But George does not only transmit experience. With his new technique, he can also convey visions —and without submerging the hearer in the word-floods of the mystics. By setting usual words in unusual combinations, he restores original lustre to concepts dulled by the repetition of every day. His language is so plastic, so three-dimensional, that even when he dares to interpolate abstract reflections without transition, he does not break the spell of the whole. The efficacy of this new manner of writing is borne out by the description of Fra Angelico's 'Coronation of Mary' (p. 41). The purity of color is conjured up by references to the yellow of wheat, the pink chalk that children use for their drawings and the indigo of women washing at the stream.

As in many works of the poet, the composition of the 'Hymns' covers the period of a year, the eternal cycle that nature and the human soul in tune with the change of the seasons require for their renewal. Driven beyond the pressure of thought by rapture and the delight in translating his spiritual intensity into words, he began to write his 'Pilgrimages' (Vienna, 1891). But these are no pious journeys to the graves of saints or to wonder-working shrines. They are agonized quests for the being who can and will understand him. He is no longer satisfied with the creatures of his imagination. Now he searches among his contemporaries for a look, for a gesture of understanding, and discovers that the secret of human companionship lies in the subtle tension through which inescapable differences are—at least temporarily—held in balance. In the poem of the mill (p. 43) he sees the procession of girls returning from Communion in silent prayer. The ice of the lake is cracking and it seems as though under the lowering burden of grey sky, dark lovers are summoning their brides into the depth.

To find an adequate expression for the pain of loneliness is the problem of this book in which the poet turns his disappointment over a friendship that did not mature into rhythms of torment and regret. He finally takes refuge in an imaginary kingdom and begins to revel in an orgy of self-destruction, a Teutonic outlet that Nietzsche was never able to give up. George, however, was saved by the memory of the clear and simple happenings of his childhood that snatch him from the slough of despond, and he grows resigned to the fact that it is still impossible for him to find a companion among the living. Once more his fantasy evokes a being, who, like himself, must create the air he can breathe in, through his own work. He tries to shape his counterpart tangibly from the odors of autumn in the island garden of Aranjuez, from the breath of dissolution, and with him he imagines a journey to a land that is everything that our earth and our everyday life is not. This counterpart is Algabal, his own interpretation of the young Roman Emperor Heliogabalus. ('Algabal,' Paris, 1892.) He boldly deviates from the historical data in the life of the sun-priest, whom, at the decline of the Roman Empire, the legionnaires, captivated by his beauty, raised on their shields as their chosen ruler. His 'Algabal' is obsessed by a sense of his own remoteness from his environment, but at the same time he shares all the passions of his people and fluctuates between a feeling of responsibility and the craving to live his life selfishly, for nothing but the fulfillment of his dreams. He builds himself a subterranean realm independent of the light and air of earth. Here he reigns as an unbridled, absolute sovereign, a doer and a dreamer, peaceful and violent with the undissipated strength of his emotions. Rather than depend on the fickle favor of the people, he plans to end his own life at the very moment in which he feels himself at odds with the force that predestines his course and drives him on. The book closes with the poem 'Augury' (p. 51). Though this is still the expression of a mood of Algabal's, it points beyond the thoughts and deeds of the emperor to the future of the poet who has already passed on to another rung of life. It would be idle to speculate as to whether the first three stanzas are intended to give the picture of the three cycles, 'Hymns, Pilgrimages and Algabal.' The only important fact is that now he has left the fantastic forest of Tusferi, of the 'incense trees,' filled with parakeets and gaudy jays, the sky is pure and swallows hover in the wind that is no longer bright and burning but cold and clear.

The poet finds a respite from the glare and fever of this verse in 'The Books of Eclogues and Eulogies, of Legends and Lays and of The Hanging Gardens' (Berlin, 1895). As though he were convalescing from a grave disease, he rediscovers the beauty of the surrounding world and his fancy turns backward through the ages to a state of early culture when man, living a shepherd's or a sailor's life (p. 55), in close accord with nature, did not strive to subdue the elements to his will. But though the setting recalls idylls, George never lapses into the jocund and playful tone of the imitators of Theocritus. Without the devices of romanticism, he paints the still unpolluted valleys and forests of his country and, in their clear and silvery atmosphere, outlines the characters of persons he has actually known. They are exalted less as individuals than for their attitude in certain crises that proved them great and single-minded in contrast with the blurring complexities of modern life. The poet knows that even they can be his companions for only a short time, but for this span at least, their paths converge with his and their very existence gives him strength.

The colors and curlicues of a Gothic town of the Middle Ages—more French than German—are the background for the 'Book of Legends and Lays.' They deal with those aspects of knighthood that sprang from timeless and universal emotions, and so are still valid in the modern world. The 'Recluse' (p. 61) epitomizes the departure of a beloved son who, lured by the deeds that life has in store for him, does not heed the entreaty to remain in a shelter that protects from the turmoil of the world. In this volume, for the first time, the poet tests the efficacy of his new language on that most difficult of undertakings: the folk-song—a current term that is frequently misunderstood, for poetry is never produced by social units, it is always the work of individuals. The more popular a poem becomes among the mass of the people, the more easily is the name of the poet forgotten. These songs (p. 63), in which the titles often form a part of the rhythmic structure, lay the foundation for the folk-songs in George's last volume of poems.

In the life-cycle of the poet, with its recurrent stages, the 'Book of The Hanging Gardens' (pp. 65-67) corresponds to the world of Algabal. It is wrong to suppose that the development of a creative artist goes forward in a straight course. It moves in ever-expanding cycles that have a common focus. Ancient Rome served to frame the figure of Algabal. Here an imagined Orient is the background for an impetuous world in which the moment is savored to the utmost and in which conquests are made for their own sake in the manner of those Oriental despots who have become legendary and are perpetuated in song. Days of joyful elation alternate with hours of brooding on the speciousness of life. Love and her kinsman Death lurk everywhere. The lord is contrasted with the liege who may have been yesterday's, who may be tomorrow's lord. But stronger than the temptation to dissolve into nothingness is the faith in conquering new realms. The Orient merely furnishes the background for present trends. The poet shifts the scene of action to a far-off land to gain the perspective he must have in order to turn very recent experiences into art. Oriental coloring pervades the landscape, but no more than sometimes happens in dreams. And at the same time, the ponds glimmering with fish, the flower beds hedged with dark thorn, the petals floating on the water, are symbols used to make the atmosphere more sensuous.

The 'Year of the Soul' (1897) continues the idea of the 'Pilgrimages.' But this time the poet's vain quest for companions is described more indirectly through visual impressions, and with a gentler melancholy. The setting of the book is an old park that breathes unbroken peace. Its tranquility emphasizes the flux in the poet's own spirit, and the same effect is produced by the contrast between the burning content of the poems and the cool and even form in which they are cast. Here the indicator of emotion is Nature. The 'Year of the Soul' begins in autumn after the harvest, as with the peoples of the South. Characteristically, that season of the year which is commonly regarded as the most suitable drop for poetry — spring — is omitted. The poems speak of an I and a You, but often these are not two people but the poet conversing with himself. Autumn is the symbol for the quiet in his soul, for the loneliness that is akin to death. The companion who timidly approached him does not entirely grasp his goals and his visions. Although he has the strength to sever a human relationship before the wane of its glory, he spares her feelings and allows her to assume a false reason for the parting. Through the winter he still takes comfort in the one bond between them: that each is imprisoned in his own loneliness like a river under a sheet of ice. Summer speeds the realization of his dream. On the far side of a stream—for the maternal element of water, reflecting, separating, always plays a role in the tense moments of his life —he sees the beckoning gesture of a friend who flings open new vistas. He could not yet have had such an experience in his own country. The air has the impalpable shimmer of the plains and shores of Belgium; this companionship is enchanting rather than permanent.

The second part of the 'Year of the Soul,' 'Dedications and Superscriptions,' contains, among others, poems that were first conceived in French (some are contained in the concluding volume of the works) and intended for a group of artists who met in Tilff near Liége, the painters Fernand Khnopff, Auguste Donnay, Armand Rassenfosse, James Ensor, and the poets, Emile Verhaeren, Charles van Lerberghe and Edmond Rassenfosse. On the whole, this part of the book speaks only of transient events. A natural pause in development is made fruitful, a phenomenon that can frequently be observed in Stefan George's creative sequence. He utilizes the respite to salvage as much of the past as possible for the future, as a support and an enrichment for his work.

The 'Year of the Soul' closes with the 'Mournful Dances' (pp. 81-89). Dance is the severance from reality, for the element of the dancer, rather than solid earth, is space that the moving body shapes to successive patterns. Through rhythmical motion, he expresses his personal elation and anguish as well as the substratum of feeling of his contemporaries. When words become the element of the dance the poet's aim is not so much the effect upon the eye as a tone sequence. Actual experience is expressed only as a means to conjure up garlands of sound. This makes everything remote from the real, and the tone of these poems has the peculiar aloofness of hymns, folk-songs and ballads. The recurrent theme is the pain of loneliness—stars and their denizens on orbits that never meet, circling to the pipes of Pan and the harmony of the spheres. The pain of being left alone, the vain search for the reasons of loneliness and the gradual wearying of sorrow itself, are caught in words. The surrounding world grows pale and unreal. Only the song, of 'the wound that once was wild' (p. 89) can see the procession of funeral torches as a picture, can hold it and probe under the dross for a spark of living fire. Sadness gives these poems their dance rhythms above the actuality of things and fuses the memories of past happiness with present pain.

The 'Tapestry of Life and The Songs of Dream and of Death with a Prelude' (1900) like many other works of the poet falls into three parts. This is more than chance or caprice: to make an object stand firm, even in the sphere of the spirit, at least three supports are necessary, and this is one of the reasons for the symbolic value of the number three in antiquity. A poet who builds up his work purposefully must weigh these matters as Dante, Homer and the great dramatists did when they planned the architecture of their magnificent word structures. Each of the three parts of the book consists of twenty-four poems, similar in form. With the experiences he had lived through up to this point, George rears a tower of stones evenly hewn, and from this point of vantage, he looks down upon the earth and the things of earth crystallize into images before his eyes. Though the outer rhythm remains the same, tranquil and animated poems alternate, and this, as well as the use of direct address, gives the work its dramatic character. The poet is no longer imprisoned in the affairs of the moment. As a stern judge, he condemns what harms, and exalts what furthers his ideals.

The 'Prelude' (pp. 91-99) proclaims his philosophy at this stage of his life. To the angel, now manifest and now intangible, he pours out his sorrows and receives consolation and guidance from one who, in the final analysis, is none other than his own soul. Laws and creeds of the outside world no longer have the power to loose and bind. The individual is the focus of this world, feeling is unified and unifies, thoughts are no longer dissipated. The individual soul has the power to rise to those elations that become rare when the early radiance of youth has dimmed. The necessary change of grief and joy is the foundation for creative activity, and does not depend on the will of the artist, it is the gift of an hour. The poet no longer seeks to shape the alien and exotic. The simplicity and austereness of the landscape of his own country are now his model. He has learned that the various moods of lyric expression are all equally valid, the song of the storm raging through the fields or that of the westwind in the laurels. This wisdom culminates in the mournful recognition that love cannot offer complete fulfillment, since the poet has as yet found no one to match his soul's strength. In the last poem of the 'Prelude' (p. 99), the poet renders a vision of his own end: no friend is near his deathbed, only the angel.

In the 'Tapestry of Life,' people and things are depicted as on the wall hangings of the Middle Ages, where the most characteristic gesture is arrested at the peak of motion and becomes ornamental against a foil in which the laws of perspective have been deliberately neglected. A wooded valley of the poet's native land (p. 101), is conceived as the primeval landscape for a toiling Adam and Eve. The monastery (p. 109) comes to be the stronghold not only of a religious, but of any spiritual form of life, for as such it functioned for many centuries in Western Europe. George symbolizes basic powers in the statues of women, each with another significant gesture. The art of the poet gives color and meaning to the yearnings of men, who, spurred on by Hope, strive toward the ever-receding blue of the distant hills and who see diamonds in tears. After the dramatic rise of the 'Prelude' and the epic harmony of the 'Tapestry,' the 'Songs of Dream and Death' supply a lyric ending. Accordingly, they are more subjective and celebrate certain occasions and persons, among them Ernest Dowson (p. 111) and Cyril Scott, for whom they were first written in English. In the 'Songs of Day and Night' (pp. 115-117), the motions of the soul are given as if in mathematical curves. The song of 'Dream and of Death' (p. 119), the last in the volume, tells of the rise of the unfettered soul. It becomes ensnared in passion, but a single call from the depth suffices to break the spell. The conflict of the powers is fused in 'the gem of flame,' calm and clear in the sky of night.

Half of the poet's life had passed. He was approaching forty when he wrote the 'Seventh Ring' (1907). His development had entered upon a new cycle and with it he had conquered new territory for his work. A thought that had at first taken shape in dreams, was transformed into flesh, for realities must exist in the realm of thought before they assume substance and so the ideas of poets are the necessary premise for every deed. After a long and vain search, George found the human being whom Nature had endowed to be his true companion. In his works, he calls this youth Maximin. In George's poems, he plays the same role as the child Beatrice for Dante. Maximin broke the spell of loneliness and the poet was convinced of the reality of his world by the fact that now another being shared it with him. When Maximin died, still young, the brief encounter had already quickened George's work with new meanings. George has told the story of this meeting in one of his rare prose passages and its significance is best conveyed by direct quotation:

'. . . When we first met Maximin in our city, he was still in his boyhood. He came toward us from under a stone arch with the unerring certainty of a young fencer, and with a look of leadership and power, softened by the mobility and vague sadness that centuries of Christian civilization have wrought in the faces of the people. In him we recognized the representative of sovereign youth, such as we had dreamed of, youth in that unbroken fulness and purity that can still move mountains and walk on dry land through the midst of the sea, youth fitted to receive our heritage and to conquer new domains. We had heard too much of the wisdom that thinks to solve the final enigma, had savored too much of the motley in the rush of impressions. The overwhelming freight of external possibilities had added nothing to the content, but the shimmering play of light had dulled the senses and slackened tensions. What we had need of, was One who was moved by plain and simple things and could show them to us, as they are beheld by the eyes of the gods . . .

'. . . Those of our contemporaries who did not see him, those who came later, will not understand how such a revelation could come from one so young. For although the sensitiveness and the prophetic splendor of the poems he left—mere fragments of a work in its beginnings—surpasses every valid standard known to us, he himself ascribed no particular importance to them, and the core of his influence will be apparent only from that which may be vouchsafed us to produce through the communion with his spirit. But we know that only sapless eras see in youth a preliminary stage and a promise, never the peak and perfection, that more in their contours than in their words and deeds, lies the lasting power of all the heroes and the mighty and those who in the grace of their spring walk the fields of summer for but a brief space, who bleed to death at the forest's verge or sink into dark waters, to be transported to heaven and to rule with deathless names over all the generations of men. We know that the great expeditions that changed the face of our world were planned by the schoolboy Alexander, that the twelve-year-old son of Galilee instructed the scribes in the capital, that the Lord of the longest world rule we know of, did not die in his thirties, but as a youth found the eternal symbols on his bloomy path, and that he died as a youth . . .

'. . . Maximin lived among us for only a short time. In accordance with a covenant that he had made in early years, he was raised to another star before he became less like gods and more like men. To the colorful and diverse destiny of a splendid mortal, he preferred the calm and quiet reign of the celestials. Even his childhood had been filled with seething divinations of the Beyond, and the struggle with One Unnamed. To Him he turned as to the only one against whom he would measure himself. Him he implored for tasks and tests and, in his yearning nights pleaded that in reward he might see the holy face. When he had learned that God could not reveal Himself in this way, he offered Him this covenant: Then let me behold you in the best of your visible creations! Give me Leda, the beloved, give me the great man, the Master! And if it is true that here every structure falls, every flame is extinguished, every flower fades, let me stand upon your summit once and then be snatched away swiftly by your eagle. . . . After these days of transport, he passed from a fevered dream to death—so quickly that we could only stare at a grave like other graves, and not believe that it contained him . . .'

The title, 'The Seventh Ring,' refers to the rings in the cross-sections of trees and indicates that the seven rings are ranged around a common focus and also that this is the seventh volume in the work of the poet. Fourteen 'Poems of Our Times' of the first ring unroll the life and work of contemporaries who represent the urges and needs of their era. In writing about those who live in our own age, it is difficult to find a point of vantage from which to make a survey. It is this that made it so hard for Goethe and Hoelderlin, for instance, to gain a poetic conception of Napoleon. George's advantage lay in the fact that through his new experience he had been removed to a spiritual level other than that of the world about him. And this, in turn, made it possible for him to see himself in relation to his own times in the person of Dante, for Dante too had found a particular position to his era with the help of a very personal experience: the meeting with Beatrice, the first true child of the new world of the Renaissance, without whom Dante's dream and work would never have been translated into reality.

The 'Frankish Lands' (p. 121) are the native land of the poet, not France but the empire of the Carolingians, that extended from the west coast of France to that part of Bavaria that is still known as Franconia. At the end of the last century, understanding for poetry and art was dead in Germany. Boecklin, the Swiss painter, had fled to Italy and Nietzsche had gone mad through the utter lack of comprehension on the part of his countrymen. George chose to live in Paris that for centuries had been a refuge for the alien and the banished. He was familiar with French culture, for he had heard the praise of France from his grandfather who spoke only French. In that country he himself met the first poets whom he recognized as such. And long after he had returned to his own country, voices from the West lured him with the tender words of the 'Song of Roland.'

In the poem 'Leo XIII' (p. 125), George celebrates the innate majesty of this Pope, whose invocation to the Christ-Child, written in Latin, he translates in the six first verses of the third stanza of his poem. In the 'Poem of Our Times,' (p. 129) he traces the specific forces that underlie the obvious repetitions in the history of his country and that are still effective. It is futile first to burden the earth with stone walls and steel framework and then to take flight in regions of mist and cloud in order to escape a soulless world. The only one who understands the law of life is he who knows that gardens turn to deserts and that only the miracle of youth endures forever.

The moving forces of the new world, and their bearers, are described in the second ring, 'Images.' The third ring is called 'Tides' (pp. 133-145), since it follows the rhythmical change between ebb and flow that pulses through the soul as through the sea. Though the majority of the experiences of which the poet speaks here belong to a cycle of his life that preceded the meeting with Maximin, they were, in part, formulated after that meeting, as a new fulness in tone betrays to the sensitive ear. The fourth ring (pp. 147-155), the core of the book, contains the elegies on Maximin, the memory of this companionship and the impassioned faith in its significance for the future. This series of poems is characterized by simplicity sustained on a high level of elation, a sharp contrast to the first three rings with their gradual rise and fall.

From the height of passionate emotion, the poet must dip back into the dark realm of dreams to gather new strength. In the fifth ring, 'Dream Darkness' (pp. 159-171), the world of tangible shapes is abandoned, even the landscape becomes unreal—it is the stuff that dreams are made of. In the sixth ring, the 'Songs' (pp. 173-179), the poet continues his experiment in the folksong. In the arrangement of the book, 'Images' and 'Songs' are placed at an equal distance from the Maximin-ring. For action conquers the territory in which the individual can run the gamut of a personal development that finally colors the feeling of a whole people and thus again becomes impersonal. And so there is an inner connection between the heroic and the lyric, between Homer and Sappho, and, for other levels of civilization between Dante and Petrarch, between the poets who sang the deeds of Dietrich von Bern, and the Minnesaenger Walther von der Vogelweide. Interestingly enough, some of the verses of the song-ring first occurred to the poet in Italian. But, as he himself explained once, to elucidate his creative process, the ideas allied to this sound were so alien to the Italian way of thinking that they called for embodiment in their proper medium. On the other hand, writing in a foreign language was no mere whim, as the layman might suppose, but meant an ultimate enrichment of phrase and ideas. His preoccupation with foreign languages culminated in adequate and beautiful translations of Shakespeare's Sonnets, of selected cantos of Dante's

30

'Divine Comedy', and of poems by Rossetti, Swinburne and the French Symbolists.

The 'Tablets,' the last part of the work, revive the original purpose of the epigram chiselled in stone, to inform later generations of important events in the most concise form possible. Their terseness, therefore, must be unembellished and independent of the purely local or temporal. Any striving for a particular effect that might obscure the prime function, should be rigorously avoided. Some of the 'Tablets' are addressed to persons, others celebrate places and events connected with them. Profiles of great poets and men of action of former times appear. In the poem to a 'Northern Master' (p. 181), George implies the secret connection between celestial splendor and earthly gloom that one finds in Rembrandt's pictures. Judgments are hurled against the laxness of contemporaries. In the 'Centenary Lines' and the 'Tempter' poems (p. 181), he reproaches his country with the fact that it has lost the feeling for its true heritage, that it no longer recognizes the truth but believes only the maddest promises of charlatans. Mournfully he foresees the gravest consequences. In the last six epigrams, the poet surveys his own work. Like Dante, he well knows that it will be significant for the course of history, and he emphasizes that the conflict and ecstasy blended in his life give his poems their characteristic movement and tone.

The 'Tapestry of Life' presents experience in a series of pictures, the 'Star of the Covenant' (1914) states it abstractly. The book consists of an 'Introit' of nine poems, three parts of thirty poems each, and a closing chorus. To mark the conclusion of a train of thought and to give a firm and unified structure, every tenth poem is rhymed. There is no division into stanzas. The number of verses in each poem varies from seven to fourteen. The book as a whole contains a thousand verses. Rhymed as well as unrhymed poems are compatible with the spirit of the German language. The choice between the two forms is not a matter of volition. It is made unconsciously from an inner compulsion to convey the seen and the felt as directly as possible. In this eighth volume of George's works, there is little poetic imagery and the rhyme which stimulates the imagination of the reader is only used where it is indispensable for the compactness of form. As in the Greek drama, language is not the means to arouse fantasy; it is an end in itself. The wisdom and the laws of the new life that are contained in this work could not be given in prose, for they are born from an intrinsic rhythm and they can be grasped through rhythm only. It is for this reason that from earliest times on, the laws according to which life is to be lived were given in rhythmical form which impresses itself on the hearer even when he listens mechanically or with reluctance. And the rhythm within the hearer adjusts to the rhythm of what is heard, and so transforms him even in body. That is why the Greeks and other peoples began the education of their children not with banal primers, but with the memorizing of the works of Homer and of those poets who shaped the national character.

The nine poems of the 'Introit' (pp. 183-185) celebrate the Maximin-experience, less in relation to the poet himself, than from the viewpoint of its significance for his whole era. In Maximin the poet sees the incarnation of sacred youth which, at intervals through the centuries, must be embodied in a single form to reunite the scattered forces. The first book deals with the poet's mission: he creates the region, the air, for the doer who will usher in a new age. He is the judge of the people to whom he is sent. He condemns the ailing spirit of the masses of today that, more blind than the so-called dark and savage centuries, deny every god in order to fashion idols according to their own desire. The poet sees the last uprising of the gods: They leave his native land, and this vision is reminiscent of Shakespeare's lines on the departure of Hercules when Mark Antony's fortunes of war change. No one, not even the wise, understood the insistent words of Nietzsche, 'the last warner' p. 195). As the teachings of Christ initiated a new era by reversing a given order, so now too, a new spiritual foundation must be laid if any future structure is to stand (p. 197). The Germans of the wintry North and the Jews, the children of the desert, are alike in that their gods are not presented in human form. Just because of their inner bond, they hate and seek one another. The same inner need forces them to wander restlessly through life, driven by the yearning to be utterly fulfilled at least once, or goaded by the fear of losing themselves completely (p. 199).

In the second book, the poet describes the repeated conflict laid upon those who try to enter the new world though they were born in the old. The third book deals with the laws and levels of the new life. These levels have nothing to do with the structure of a man-made society. The leading spirits among men are not class-bound, but emerge sporadically from any stratum of the nation. True inner nobility has nothing to do with the current concept of aristocracy (p. 213). Thought and action are no longer separated: they are fused and directed to a common goal and maintained by the power of faith. A new generation of youth does not squander its strength, for it divines the need of all reserves in the coming struggle. The book ends in a paean, a chorus, which is not the expression of a single soul, but the voice of a welded throng (p. 215).

George published his last work in 1928. From then until his death, he deliberately desisted from writing poetry. The laws of the new life had been given in the 'Star of the Covenant.' The forms of this life are reflected in the 'Kingdom Come.' Here the architectural build of his former works seemed to impose too many restrictions. This work is like a bold stone bridge flung across a broad current. It has no formal subdivisions. The book begins with evocations of the poet's spiritual forebears, Goethe and Hoelderlin, who, although he loved his country, did not hesitate to expose the weaknesses of his contemporaries in Hyperion's letters to Bellarmin. In George's poem (p. 217), Hoelderlin is alien to his own times. He knows that only through blood-sacrifice can the Greek miracle of transmitting wisdom and art to the next generation be regained, that he himself is destined to be a victim before the prime of his life. His reward is a clear grasp of the present and a profound presentiment of the future. In the poem 'The War,' published as a pamphlet during the war of 1914-1918, which the poet even as early as 1921 called the 'first world war,' he already foresees the luckless ending for his people: that puppet kings and traders cannot unravel the reel of this earth; that the old field marshal at the head of hosts could find the solution for the hour but would not be able to save the country from worse foes within. In such times of transition, the poet functions as a prophet. It is his charge to guard the flame of the spirit until this spirit shapes bodies for itself, until a new generation arises that does not lie, that despises the profession of pretended unity, and Here and Now makes real the Kingdom Come.

The other long poems of this volume approach the hymn of antiquity. Their purpose is not to describe the factual, but to produce an ecstasy of sound that transfigures the factual and raises it to a sphere of national and religious community of feeling. The subjective zone of lyric poetry is forsaken; the ego no longer is the universe, it merges in it. The 'conversations' in this volume: 'The Hanged, Man and Faun, The Lord and the Centurion, The Burning of the Temple,' have a dramatic core, not in the sense that action visibly takes place as in the drama of the Christian era, but rather as in the drama of antiquity where after the event, bearers of different views of living are brought face to face and develop their emotions and thoughts in statement and response. The hunter encounters the faun, the spirit of the woods (p. 221). The man no longer recognizes the forces of nature that the faun represents. What is and has always been, he regards as a monstrosity because it does not fit into his human thought that is already remote from nature and her workings. He scorns the power embodied by the faun whenever he meets with it in life, but in his prayers he invokes it tremblingly and does not know that the gods reveal themselves only through go-betweens. He does not want to admit to himself that the fruitfulness on which all human life depends cannot be traced back to something explicable by reason.

The 'Verses to Friends, Living and Dead) (pp. 227-231), characterized by directness and simplicity, constitute a return from the universal to the personal. They are followed by songs that are folk-songs in the sense that they express the fluctuant yearning of mankind. In the youth of a people, poetry is the rhythmic magic through which the help of the god is enlisted. Then it becomes epic and records the deed of divine and human ancestors. Relatively late the individual begins to sing his personal joys and sorrows—lyric poetry is born. It is classic as long as it strives to mould the soul to the patterns of antiquity, and it turns romantic when individual pain grows into undefined

35

sadness about the ways of the world. The culmination of romantic poetry is the folk-song which voices the simplest and most profound feeling of the people and makes it tangible in the guise of an every-day occurrence. The song of the soul that does not know whence it comes or whither it will go, is written in terza rima (p. 233). The loneliness of an aging heart expresses itself in the yearning for the blond child that appears on the beach at sunset (p. 235). The deed alone is not enough; it acquires creative force only when the word that designates it has been found. The concluding poem of the volume (p. 245) tells of a flawless and slender flame that shines victorious in consuming passion. It is preceded by the two last poems George wrote (pp. 241-243): about a sweet and burning light that drives even the steadfast soul hard to the abyss.

O N DECEMBER 4, 1933, Stefan George died in voluntary exile at the Lago Maggiore. The Swiss sculptor Uehlinger made a cast of his hands and two death masks which have not yet been released to the public. The Nazi government wished to take his body to his native land and to inter him with great solemnity in one of the famous medieval cathedrals, but this was refused by the few close friends who had been called to Locarno. They carried his body to a small chapel where the peasants gather for funerals, and without any publicity, buried him in the early morning. He lies in the cemetery of Minusio. The grey slab of Alpine granite bears only his name in the script he himself evolved and used for his works.

Ernst Morwitz

Stefan George

POEMS

STRAND

O lenken wir hinweg von wellenauen!
Die, wenn auch wild im wollen und mit düsterm rollen
Nur dulden scheuer möven schwingenschlag
Und stet des keuschen himmels farben schauen.
Wir heuchelten zu lang schon vor dem tag.

Zu weihern grün mit moor und blumenspuren
Wo gras und laub und ranken wirr und üppig
        schwanken
Und ewger abend einen altar weiht!
Die schwäne die da aus der buchtung fuhren,
Geheimnisreich, sind unser brautgeleit.

Die lust entführt uns aus dem fahlen norden:
Wo deine lippen glühen fremde kelche blühen—
Und fliesst dein leib dahin wie blütenschnee
Dann rauschen alle stauden in akkorden
Und werden lorbeer tee und aloe.

STRAND

O let us leave the meadows of the sea!
That in their savage reign and sombre surf sustain
Only the tameless gulls in winging sway,
And lave the virgin heavens endlessly.
Too long we made pretense before the day.

To emerald pond with marsh and bloomy trail,
Where grass and vines and leaves are rocked in tangled
      sheaves,
Eternal eve a holy altar wreathed!
The swans that out of yonder inlet sail
Are escort to the bride, in secret sheathed.

Delight has snatched us from the fallow fjords,
Where your lips are aglow, exotic flowers blow—
And when your flesh as snowbloom melts away,
Then all the stalks begin to surge in chords
And turn to aloe, tea and sprays of bay.

EIN ANGELICO

Auf zierliche kapitel der legende
—Den erdenstreit bewacht von ewgem rat,
Des strengen ahnen wirkungsvolle sende—
Errichtet er die glorreich grosse tat:

Er nahm das gold von heiligen pokalen,
Zu hellem haar das reife weizenstroh,
Das rosa kindern die mit schiefer malen,
Der wäscherin am bach den indigo.

Der herr im glanze reinen königtumes
Zur seite sanfte sänger seines ruhmes
Und sieger der Chariten und Medusen.

Die braut mit immerstillem kindesbusen
Voll demut aber froh mit ihrem lohne
Empfängt aus seiner hand die erste krone.

AN ANGELICO

Above the graceful headings of the story
—Eternal vigil over man who strives,
The ruthless sire's message full of glory—
The deed of glowing grandeur he contrives:

The gold from holy chalices he took,
For yellow hair, the ripened wheaten stalks,
The blue from women washing at the brook,
The pink from children coloring with chalks.

The Lord in kingship's pure and lustrous frame,
Beside Him gentle singers of His fame,
And victors of Medusas, friends of Graces,

The bride whose childish breathing never races,
So meek, and yet with her reward enchanted,
A crown—her very first—by Him is granted.

Mühle lass die arme still
Da die haide ruhen will.
Teiche auf den tauwind harren,
Ihrer pflegen lichte lanzen
Und die kleinen bäume starren
Wie getünchte ginsterpflanzen.

Weisse kinder schleifen leis
Ueberm see auf blindem eis
Nach dem segentag, sie kehren
Heim zum dorf in stillgebeten,
DIE beim fernen gott der lehren,
DIE schon bei dem naherflehten.

Kam ein pfiff am grund entlang?
Alle lampen flackern bang.
War es nicht als ob es riefe?
Es empfingen ihre bräute
Schwarze knaben aus der tiefe . .
Glocke läute glocke läute!

Stay your arms, O turning mill,
For the heath would now be still.
Ponds before the thaw are glooming
Rimmed with shining lance for lance,
And the little trees are looming
Like the varnished woodwax plants.

On the blind and frozen tide
Whiteclad children softly glide
Homeward from Communion, pray
Mutely: these to God whom learning
Rendered far aloof, and they
To the One who yields to yearning.

Did a whistle shrill below?
All the candles faintly flow.
Was it not like voices calling?
Ebon boys in deepness bound
Drew their brides into their thralling . . .
Bell, resound, O bell, resound!

Ihr alten bilder schlummert mit den toten,
Euch zu erwecken mangelt mir die macht,
Die wahren auen wurden mir verboten,
Nun kost ich an verderbnisvoller pracht.

Getroffen von berauschenden gerüchten
Erblick ich in dem blauen wiesental
Die reiher weiss und rosafarben flüchten
Zum nahen see der schläft und glänzt wie stahl.

Da schritt sie wie im ebenmass der klänge,
Ihr hochgestreckter finger hielt und hob
Der bergenden gewänder seidenstränge
Die sie bei nacht aus weidenflocken wob.

O weises spiel durch diese hüllen ahnen!
In meinen sinnen blieben wir ein paar
Bevor sie hinter blumigen lianen
Zum nahen see hinabgeglitten war.

You ancient visions with the dead have vanished,
I lack the strength to conjure you again,
Since from the true dominions I was banished,
I now will taste the splendor tinged with bane.

By rumors of enchantment I am stricken:
The meadows of an azure vale reveal
How herons white and rosy-colored quicken
The nearby lake that sleeps and shines as steel.

There, as in symmetry of chords she paces,
Her upward pointed finger lifts and takes
The shrouding garment by its silken laces,
That in the night she wove of willow flakes.

O subtle play divined behind these veilings!
My senses wrought the fancy we were paired,
Before through vines that screen with bloomy trailings
Down to the nearby lake she slowly fared.

Beträufelt an baum und zaun
Ein balsam das sprocke holz?
Verspäteter sonnen erglühn
Die herbstlichen farben verschmolz
Rotgelb, gesprenkeltes braun
Scharlach und seltsames grün.

Wer naht sich dem namenlosen
Der fern von der menge sich härmt?
In mattblauen kleidern ein kind . .
So raschelt ein schüchterner wind
So duften sterbende rosen
Von scheidenden strahlen erwärmt.

An schillernder hecken rand
Bei dorrenden laubes geknister
Und lichter wipfel sang
Führen wir uns bei der hand
Wie märchenhafte geschwister
Verzückt und mit zagendem gang.

What balm on brittle bark
Of fence and tree is oozed?
The sun with an ultimate sheen
The colors of fall interfused:
Redgold, a stipple of dark,
Scarlet and curious green.

Who turns to the yet unknown
Remote in his grief from the swarm?
In dim blue attire, a child . . .
So rustles a wind flowing mild,
From faded roses is blown
Such scent when the sun is still warm.

By shimmering hedges' row,
Through surge of the withering trails
And songs of lighted sprays,
Clinging together we go
Like fabled siblings in tales,
And falter with spell-dazzled gaze.

Der saal des gelben gleisses und der sonne.
Sie herrscht auf flacher kuppel unter sternen,
In blitzen schnellen aus dem feuerbronne
Topase untermengt mit bernstein-kernen.

An allen seiten aufgereiht als spiegel
—Gesamter städte ganzer staaten beute—
Die ungeschmückten platten goldnen ziegel
Und an der erde breiten löwenhäute.

Nur nicht des Einen scharfen blick zu blenden
Vermag die stechend grelle weltenkrone
Und dreimal tausend schwere urnen spenden
Den geist von amber weihrauch und zitrone.

The hall of yellow radiance and of sun,
On level dome among the stars he reigns,
And from the fiery well in flashes run
Topazes interfused with amber grains.

On every side as mirrors ranged in files
—Entire towns' and kingdoms' plundered store—
Are flat and unembellished golden tiles,
And lion skins are broad upon the floor.

Only to blind the piercing gaze of Him
The dazzling crown of worlds does not suffice,
And thrice a thousand heavy vessels brim
With breath of citron, ambergris and spice.

VOGELSCHAU

Weisse schwalben sah ich fliegen,
Schwalben schnee- und silberweiss,
Sah sie sich im winde wiegen,
In dem winde hell und heiss.

Bunte häher sah ich hüpfen,
Papagei und kolibri
Durch die wunder-bäume schlüpfen
In dem wald der Tusferi.

Grosse raben sah ich flattern,
Dohlen schwarz und dunkelgrau
Nah am grunde über nattern
Im verzauberten gehau.

Schwalben seh ich wieder fliegen,
Schnee- und silberweisse schar,
Wie sie sich im winde wiegen
In dem winde kalt und klar!

AUGURY

White I saw the swallows winging,
Swallows snow- and silver-white,
In the wind I saw them clinging,
In the burning wind and bright.

Jays I saw that slipped and shimmered,
Parakeet and colibri
Through the trees of wonder glimmered,
In the wood of Tusferi.

Huge I saw the ravens slacken,
Daws of black and sombre grey,
Over adders, near the bracken,
Where the magic timber lay.

Now again I see the winging
Snow and silver swallows veer,
In the wind I see them clinging,
In the freezing wind and clear!

JAHRESTAG

O schwester nimm den krug aus grauem ton,
Begleite mich! denn du vergassest nicht
Was wir in frommer wiederholung pflegten.
Heut sind es sieben sommer dass wirs hörten
Als wir am brunnen schöpfend uns besprachen:
Uns starb am selben tag der bräutigam.
Wir wollen an der quelle wo zwei pappeln
Mit einer fichte in den wiesen stehn
Im krug aus grauen thone wasser holen.

ANNIVERSARY

O Sister, take the jug of sallow clay
And come with me, for you have not forgot
What in devout renewal still we cherish.
Now it is seven summers since they told us,
While at the well we talked and fetched the water:
That on the selfsame day our bridegrooms died.
There on the meadow where a pine is growing
Beside two poplars, let us fill our jugs
Of sallow clay with water from the fountain.

DER TAG DES HIRTEN

Die herden trabten aus den winterlagern.
Ihr junger hüter zog nach langer frist
Die ebne wieder die der fluss erleuchtet,
Die froh-erwachten äcker grüssten frisch,
Ihm riefen singende gelände zu,
Er aber lächelte für sich und ging
Voll neuer ahnung auf den frühlingswegen.
Er übersprang mit seinem stab die furt
Und hielt am andern ufer wo das gold
Von leiser flut aus dem geröll gespült
Ihn freute und die bunten vielgestalten
Und zarten muscheln deuteten ihm glück.
Er hörte nicht mehr seiner lämmer blöken
Und wanderte zum wald zur kühlen schlucht,
Da stürzen steile bäche zwischen felsen
Auf denen moose tropfen und entblösst
Der buchen schwarze wurzeln sich verästen.
Im schweigen und erschauern dichter wipfel
Entschlief er während hoch die sonne stand
Und in den wassern schnellten silberschuppen.
Er klomm erwacht zu berges haupt und kam
Zur feier bei des lichtes weiterzug,
Er krönte betend sich mit heilgem laub
Und in die lind bewegten lauen schatten
Schon dunkler wolken drang sein lautes lied.

SHEPHERD'S DAY

The herds were trotting from their winter quarters,
Their young attendant after many moons
Across the river-brightened meadows wandered
Again, the fields awoke serene and fresh
And regions called to him with melodies.
But smiling to himself he walked the paths
Of springtide and was filled with new divining.
The ford he vaulted with his staff and stood
Upon the further landing where the gold
From stony rubble washed by gentle waves,
Rejoiced him, and the divers-shaped, the motley
And fragile shells foretold his happiness.
The bleating of his lambs he heard no longer,
And wandered to the wood, the frosty glen.
There plunging streams are steep between the boulders
On which the mosses drip, and bared and black,
The roots of beeches branch. Beneath the silence
And gentle tremors in the arching treetops,
He fell asleep while still the sun was high,
And silver scales were darting through the waters.
Awakened, up the peak he climbed and reached
The festive rite of onward flowing light.
He prayed and crowned himself with sacred leaves,
And to the warm and slowly drifted shadows
Of darkened clouds, his ringing song arose.

ABEND DES FESTES

Nimm auch von deinem haupt den kranz, Menech-
    tenus!
Entfernen wir uns eh der flöten ton entschläft,
Zwar reicht man ehrend uns noch frohe becher dar,
Doch seh ich mitleid schon durch manchen trunknen
    blick.
Wir beide wurden von den priestern nicht erwählt
Zur schar die sühnend in dem tempel wirken darf.
Von allen zwölfen waren wir allein nicht schön
Und dennoch sagte uns die quelle deine stirn
Und meine schulter seien reinstes elfenbein.
Wir können mit den schäfern nicht mehr weiden gehn
Und mit den pflügern nicht mehr an der furche hin
Die wir das werk der himmlischen zu tun gelernt.
Gib deinen kranz! ich schleudr' ihn mit dem meinen
    weg,
Ergreifen wir auf diesem leeren pfad die flucht,
Verirren wir uns in des schwarzen schicksals wald.

AFTER THE FESTIVAL

Take from your head the garland too, Menechtenus,
And let us go before the sound of flutes is lulled.
Though still they offer cups of joy to honor us,
I see compassion break through many a reeling gaze.
We two were not elected by the priests to those
Who are allowed to expiate within the shrine.
Of all the twelve we only were not beautiful,
And none the less the waves apprize us that your brow,
And that my shoulders are of purest ivory.
No longer with the shepherds can we go afield,
And with the ploughers walk the furrows' length no
      more,
We, who have learned to ply the handicraft of gods.
Give me your garland! I shall fling it far with mine.
Along this empty path let us escape in flight,
And let us lose our way in woods of sombre Fate.

AN APOLLONIA

Traue dem glück! lacht es auch heut, Apollonia, nicht.
Nötiger schmerz blich dein gesicht, doch es zeigt dass
    du bald
Schmiegsam und stark über ihn siegst, nie mehr lohe
    dann glut,
Rüttle dann sturm an deinem haus, nie mehr walte das
    spiel
Wo unser fuss wange und hand gar zu nah sich gefühlt.
Göttin und welt, gattin des Tros der mich brüderlich
    liebt,
Den du erhobst als er zu sehr Pirras halber geklagt!
Fern will ich sein: richtest du neu glänzend blühend
    dich auf,
Gemmen dein aug, kirschen dein mund, reife halme
    dein haar.

TO APOLLONIA

Trust in your Fate! though it be grave, Apollonia,
    today,
Needful distress whitened your face, but it shows that
    you will
Vanquish it soon, supple and strong, then no longer
    shall flame
Leap nor the storm totter your house, then no longer
    shall play
Rule when our feet, temples and hands, both too close
    we have felt.
Goddess and world, wedded to Tros, who like kin is
    to me,
Whom you upraised when he had mourned over Pirra
    too much!
Far would I be: when you revive, glowing, flower-
    ing, new,
Jewels your eyes, cherries your mouth, wheat full-
    ripened your hair.

DER EINSIEDEL

Ins offne fenster nickten die hollunder
Die ersten reben standen in der bluht,
Da kam mein sohn zurück vom land der wunder,
Da hat mein sohn an meiner brust geruht.

Ich liess mir allen seinen kummer beichten,
Gekränkten stolz auf seinem erden-ziehn—
Ich hätte ihm so gerne meinen leichten
Und sichern frieden hier bei mir verliehn.

Doch anders fügten es der himmel sorgen—
Sie nahmen nicht mein reiches lösegeld . .
Er ging an einem jungen ruhmes-morgen,
Ich sah nur fern noch seinen schild im feld.

THE RECLUSE

The elders through the open window swayed,
The vines already into blossom pressed,
Then home my son from lands of wonder strayed,
My son then lay at rest upon my breast.

I let him tell the tale of all his woe,
In earthly farings all his wounded pride—
I should have liked so much to have him know
The calm and poised secureness at my side.

But other goals the cares of heaven frame—
Though rich my ransom, they refused to yield . . .
He left upon a morning young with fame,
I watched his shield move through the distant field.

Sieh mein kind ich gehe.
Denn du darfst nicht kennen
Nicht einmal durch nennen
Menschen müh und wehe.

Mir ist um dich bange.
Sieh mein kind ich gehe
Dass auf deiner wange
Nicht der duft verwehe.

Würde dich belehren,
Müsste dich versehren
Und das macht mir wehe.
Sieh mein kind ich gehe.

See my child, I leave,
You must not behold,
No, nor yet be told
How men toil and grieve.

Over you I gloom,
See my child, I leave,
That as yester, bloom
On your cheek may weave.

I should make you wise,
I should wake your sighs.
And that makes me grieve,
See my child, I leave.

Hain in diesen paradiesen
Wechselt ab mit blütenwiesen
Hallen, buntbemalten fliesen.
Schlanker störche schnäbel kräuseln
Teiche die von fischen schillern,
Vögel-reihen matten scheines
Auf den schiefen firsten trillern
Und die goldnen binsen säuseln—
Doch mein traum verfolgt nur eines.

Saget mir auf welchem pfade
Heute sie vorüberschreite—
Dass ich aus der reichsten lade
Zarte seidenweben hole,
Rose pflücke und viole,
Dass ich meine wange breite,
Schemel unter ihrer sohle.

Forests in these Edens flow
Into fields of blossom snow,
Painted tiles and portico.
Beaks of slender storks are curling
Ponds that fish have streaked with glamor,
Rows of birds in tarnished hues
From the crooked ridges clamor,
And the golden reeds are purling—
Yet my dream but This pursues.

Tell me on what path today
She will come and wander by—
That from treasure chest I may
Lift a web that silken blows,
Violet gather and the rose,
That I lean my cheek to lie
Underfoot for her repose.

Das schöne beet betracht ich mir im harren,
Es ist umzäunt mit purpurn-schwarzem dorne
Drin ragen kelche mit geflecktem sporne
Und sammtgefiederte geneigte farren
Und flockenbüschel wassergrün und rund
Und in der mitte glocken weiss und mild—
Von einem odem ist ihr feuchter mund
Wie süsse frucht vom himmlischen gefild.

Du lehnest wider eine silberweide
Am ufer, mit des fächers starren spitzen
Umschirmest du das haupt dir wie mit blitzen
Und rollst als ob du spieltest dein geschmeide.
Ich bin im boot das laubgewölbe wahren
In das ich dich vergeblich lud zu steigen . .
Die weiden seh ich die sich tiefer neigen
Und blumen die verstreut im wasser fahren.

Fair-bedded blooms in waiting I discern,
By thorns of black and purple they are hedged,
There cups are looming, spurred and dapple-fledged,
And velvet-crested, over-leaning fern.
And flaky clusters watergreen and wreathed
And in the middle white and gentle bells—
A fragrance from their dewy mouth is breathed
Like fruit that sweetens in celestial dells.

Against a silver willow on the shore
You leaned and with your fan you framed your hair,
The pointed slats in flashes seemed to flare
And as in play you twirled the gems you wore.
Down to my boat that leafen arches hide
I vainly had implored you to descend . . .
I saw the boughs of willow lower bend
And scattered blossoms on the water glide.

Komm in den totgesagten park und schau:
Der schimmer ferner lächelnder gestade,
Der reinen wolken unverhofftes blau
Erhellt die weiher und die bunten pfade.

Dort nimm das tiefe gelb, das weiche grau
Von birken und von buchs, der wind ist lau,
Die späten rosen welkten noch nicht ganz,
Erlese küsse sie und flicht den kranz,

Vergiss auch diese lezten astern nicht,
Den purpur um die ranken wilder reben
Und auch was übrig blieb von grünem leben
Verwinde leicht im herbstlichen gesicht.

Come to the park they say is dead, and view
The shimmer of the smiling shores beyond,
The stainless clouds with unexpected blue
Diffuse a light on motley path and pond.

The tender grey, the burning yellow seize
Of birch and boxwood, mellow is the breeze.
Not wholly do the tardy roses wane,
So kiss and gather them and wreathe the chain.

The purple on the twists of wilding vine,
The last of asters you shall not forget,
And what of living verdure lingers yet,
Around the autumn vision lightly twine.

Nun säume nicht die gaben zu erhaschen
Des scheidenden gepränges vor der wende,
Die grauen wolken sammeln sich behende,
Die nebel können bald uns überraschen.

Ein schwaches flöten von zerpflücktem aste
Verkündet dir dass lezte güte weise
Das land—eh es im nahen sturm vereise—
Noch hülle mit beglänzendem damaste.

Die wespen mit den goldengrünen schuppen
Sind von verschlossnen kelchen fortgeflogen,
Wir fahren mit dem kahn in weitem bogen
Um bronzebraunen laubes inselgruppen.

Now do not lag in reaching for the boon
Of parting pomp before the turn of tide,
The clouds of grey together swiftly glide,
Perhaps the mist will fall upon us soon.

From scattered bough a faint and fluting phrase
Betrays to you that goodness, wise and last,
—Before the storm impends with icy blast—
Around the land a sheen of damask lays.

The wasps with scales of golden-green have gone
From folded cups of flowers, and we swerve
Within our boat in widely sweeping curve
Around the isles of leaves in bronze and fawn.

Wo die strahlen schnell verschleissen
Leichentuch der kahlen auen,
Wasser sich in furchen stauen
In den sümpfen schmelzend gleissen

Und zum strom vereinigt laufen:
Türm ich für erinnerungen
Spröder freuden die zersprungen
Und für dich den scheiterhaufen.

Weg den schritt vom brande lenkend
Greif ich in dem boot die ruder—
Drüben an dem strand ein bruder
Winkt das frohe banner schwenkend.

Tauwind fährt in ungestümen
Stössen über brache schollen,
Mit den welken seelen sollen
Sich die pfade neu beblümen.

Where the beams are swiftly slashing
Pall of death on barren land,
Waters in the furrows stand,
In the mires melted, flashing

And united seek the river:
Pyres here for you I light
And for memories of slight
Pleasures that to fragments shiver.

From the fires onward flinging
In the boat I seize an oar—
There a brother on the shore
Waves, the happy banner swinging.

Winds of thaw are swept in powered
Gusts across the fallow plain,
With the withered souls again
Shall the paths be overflowered.

Gemahnt dich noch das schöne bildnis dessen
Der nach den schluchten-rosen kühn gehascht,
Der über seiner jagd den tag vergessen,
Der von der dolden vollem seim genascht?

Der nach dem parke sich zur ruhe wandte,
Trieb ihn ein flügelschillern allzuweit,
Der sinnend sass an jenes weihers kante
Und lauschte in die tiefe heimlichkeit . .

Und von der insel moosgekrönter steine
Verliess der schwan das spiel des wasserfalls
Und legte in die kinderhand die feine
Die schmeichelnde den schlanken hals.

Have you his lovely image still in mind,
Who boldly at the chasm's roses caught,
Who passing day forgot in such a find,
Who heavy nectar from the clusters sought?

Who when the sheen of wings had driven him
Too far, for resting turned into the park,
Who musing sat at yonder water's rim
And listened to the deep and secret dark . . .

The swan by falling waters left his stand,
His island built of stones that mosses deck,
And laid within a child's caressing hand,
And delicate—his slender neck.

Des sehers wort ist wenigen gemeinsam:
Schon als die ersten kühnen wünsche kamen
In einem seltnen reiche ernst und einsam
Erfand er für die dinge eigne namen—

Die hier erdonnerten von ungeheuern
Befehlen oder lispelten wie bitten,
Die wie Paktolen in rubinenfeuern
Und bald wie linde frühlingsbäche glitten,

An deren kraft und klang er sich ergezte,
Sie waren wenn er sich im höchsten schwunge
Der welt entfliehend unter träume sezte
Des tempels saitenspiel und heilge zunge.

Nur sie—und nicht der sanften lehre lallen,
Das mütterliche—hat er sich erlesen
Als er im rausch von mai und nachtigallen
Sann über erster sehnsucht fabelwesen,

Als er zum lenker seiner lebensfrühe
Im beten rief ob die verheissung löge . .
Erflehend dass aus zagen busens mühe
Das denkbild sich zur sonne heben möge.

The word of seers is not for common sharing:
Within a kingdom lone and strange and grave,
When first his wishes roused him with their daring,
The names that he had found, to things he gave—

That here with vast commands, with thunder teemed,
Or sounded as the faltering of desires,
That now like brooks of spring serenely streamed,
And like Pactolus now in ruby fires,

And that with might and music were his slaking.
They were, when in abandonment he flung
Himself aloft to dreams, the world forsaking,
The temple's lyre and its holy tongue.

They were the choice that he had made—away
From gently murmured mother precepts turning—
When all entranced by nightingales and May
He mused on fabled things of early yearning.

When to the guide of his awakening praying
He asked if promise had been fraught with lies . . .
And pleaded that from timid breast's essaying
The bodied image to the sun arise.

REIFEFREUDEN

Ein stolzes beben und ein reiches schallen
Durch später erde schwere fülle strich . .
Die kurzen worte waren kaum gefallen
Als tiefer rührung ruhe uns beschlich.

Sie sanken hin wo sich am fruchtgeländer
Der purpurschein im gelben schmelz verlor,
Sie stiegen auf zum schmuck der hügelränder
Wo für die dunkle lust die traube gor.

Ich wagte dir nicht, du nicht mir zu nahen
Als schräger strahl um unsre häupter schoss,
Noch gar mit rede störend zu bejahen
Was jezt uns band, was jedes stumm genoss

Und was in uns bei jenes tages rüste
Auf zu den veilchenfarbnen wolken klomm:
Was mehr als unsre träume und gelüste
An diesem gluten-abend zart erglomm.

RIPENING

A lofty tremor and a lavish song
Through autumn earth in heavy splendor strayed . . .
The sparing words had not been spoken long
When hush of deep emotion held us swayed.

Where purple flames in yellow glory merge,
Beside the trellis hung with fruit, they fell,
They mounted to the vineyard's jewelled verge
Where clustered grapes for dark desire swell.

I dared not cling to you nor you to me,
When slanting rays were loosed upon our brow,
Nor yet affirm in clumsy words what we
In silent gladness felt, what bound us now,

And what in us, when day had shed its beams,
Up to the violet-colored clouds arose,
What more than all our cravings and our dreams
Was softly kindled on that eve of glows.

Es lacht in dem steigenden jahr dir
Der duft aus dem garten noch leis.
Flicht in dem flatternden haar dir
Eppich und ehrenpreis.

Die wehende saat ist wie gold noch,
Vielleicht nicht so hoch mehr und reich,
Rosen begrüssen dich hold noch,
Ward auch ihr glanz etwas bleich.

Verschweigen wir was uns verwehrt ist,
Geloben wir glücklich zu sein
Wenn auch nicht mehr uns beschert ist
Als noch ein rundgang zu zwein.

The tides of the year for you breathe still
From gardens a smiling perfume,
Fluttering locks for you wreathe still
Ivy and speedwell bloom.

Like gold is the wavering wheat now,
No more perhaps lavish and high,
Roses in loveliness greet now,
Albeit their radiance went by.

So let us conceal what we miss, then,
And vow to be happy again,
Though no more be granted but this, then:
A round to be gone by us twain.

Dies leid und diese last: zu bannen
Was nah erst war und mein.
Vergebliches die arme spannen
Nach dem was nur mehr schein,

Dies heilungslose sich betäuben
Mit eitlem nein und kein,
Dies unbegründete sich sträuben,
Dies unabwendbar-sein.

Beklemmendes gefühl der schwere
Auf müd gewordner pein,
Dann dieses dumpfe weh der leere,
O dies: mit mir allein!

This burden and this grief: to ban
My once so close and own,
In vain with reaching arms to span
What now—a wraith—is flown.

This dulling without cure or stay,
With idle no and none,
This groundless rising up at bay,
This course that must be run.

The weighing sorrows that oppress
An anguish weary grown,
This numbing pain of emptiness,
This: with myself alone!

Keins wie dein feines ohr
Merkt was tief innen singt,
Was noch so schüchtern schwingt,
Was halb sich schon verlor.

Keins wie dein festes wort
Sucht so bestimmt den trost
In dem was wir erlost,
Des wahren friedens hort.

Keins wie dein fromm gemüt
Bespricht so leicht den gram . .
Der eines abends nahm
Was uns im tag geglüht.

None but your subtle ear
Marks what deep inward sings,
What O so shyly swings,
What half no more we hear.

None but your steady phrase
The balm so well can seize
In what our lot decrees:
A trove of peaceful ways.

None but your pious thought
So lightly speaks of pain . . .
That once at dusk could drain
The glow our day had brought.

Der hügel wo wir wandeln liegt im schatten,
Indes der drüben noch im lichte webt
Der mond auf seinen zarten grünen matten
Nur erst als kleine weisse wolke schwebt.

Die strassen weithin-deutend werden blasser,
Den wandrern bietet ein gelispel halt,
Ist es vom berg ein unsichtbares wasser
Ist es ein vogel der sein schlaflied lallt?

Der dunkelfalter zwei die sich verfrühten
Verfolgen sich von halm zu halm im scherz . .
Der rain bereitet aus gesträuch und blüten
Den duft des abends für gedämpften schmerz.

The hill where we are roaming lies in shadow,
While that beyond is all enmeshed in light,
The moon within her green and tender meadow
Is still a little cloud, adrift and white.

The roads that point afar, are slowly paling,
The wand'rers have been stayed by whispered sighs,
Is it a hidden stream from mountains trailing,
Is it a bird that quavers hushabyes?

Two moths that flew abroad before their hour
Are playing at pursuit from leaf to leaf,
The meadow's edge distills from bush and flower
The scent of evening for a muted grief.

Da vieles wankt und blasst und sinkt und splittert
Erstirbt das lied von dunst und schlaf umflutet
Bis jäher stoss das mürbe laub zerknittert,
Von ehmals wilde wunde wieder blutet—

Bis plötzlich sonne zuckt aus nassen wettern,
Ein schwarzer fluss die bleichen felder spreitet
Und seltne donner durch die fröste schmettern . .
Es merkt nur in dem zug der grabwärts gleitet

Die fackeln zwischen den geneigten nacken,
Der klänge dröhnen aus dem trauerprunke
Und sucht ob unter rauhen leides schlacken
Noch glimme ewig klarer freude funke.

Since much is wan and torn and sinks and quivers,
The song is dead in flood of mist and dreaming,
Till sudden gust the brittle foliage shivers,
The wound that once was wild, again is streaming.

Till breaking sun through wet of weathers flashes,
And black, a river spans the pallid plain,
And through the frosts a seldom thunder crashes . . .
It marks but in the graveward gliding train

The clangor from sepulchral splendor pouring,
The torches held among the bended shoulders,
And asks if under dross of harsh deploring
The clear eternal spark of joy still smoulders.

Ich forschte bleichen eifers nach dem horte
Nach strofen drinnen tiefste kümmerniss
Und dinge rollten dumpf und ungewiss—
Da trat ein nackter engel durch die pforte:

Entgegen trug er dem versenkten sinn
Der reichsten blumen last und nicht geringer
Als mandelblüten waren seine finger
Und rosen rosen waren um sein kinn.

Auf seinem haupte keine krone ragte
Und seine stimme fast der meinen glich:
Das schöne leben sendet mich an dich
Als boten: während er dies lächelnd sagte

Entfielen ihm die lilien und mimosen—
Und als ich sie zu heben mich gebückt
Da kniet auch ER, ich badete beglückt
Mein ganzes antlitz in den frischen rosen.

For treasure, pale with passion once I peered,
For verses fraught with sorrow most profound,
With things that moved in vague and stolid round—
When through the gate a naked angel neared:

And to the mind that was submerged within
He bore a bloomy load of richest dower,
No less his fingers were than almond flower,
And roses, roses were around his chin.

No coronet was set upon his head,
And to my own his voice was nearly true:
From Life where beauty rules, I come to you
As herald: and while smiling this he said,

The lilies and mimosa from him spilled—
And when to gather them I bended low,
He also knelt, with happiness aglow
In fresh-blown roses all my face I stilled.

Gib mir den grossen feierlichen hauch
Gib jene glut mir wieder die verjünge
Mit denen einst der kindheit flügelschwünge
Sich hoben zu dem frühsten opferrauch.

Ich mag nicht atmen als in deinem duft.
Verschliess mich ganz in deinem heiligtume!
Von deinem reichen tisch nur eine krume!
So fleh ich heut aus meiner dunklen kluft.

Und ER: was jezt mein ohr so stürmisch trifft
Sind wünsche die sich unentwirrbar streiten.
Gewährung eurer vielen kostbarkeiten
Ist nicht mein amt, und meine ehrengift

Wird nicht im zwang errungen, dies erkenn!
Ich aber bog den arm an seinen knieen
Und aller wachen sehnsucht stimmen schrieen:
Ich lasse nicht, du segnetest mich denn.

Give me again the solemn breath and great,
Give me the blaze again that renders young,
With which the wings of childhood once were swung
To earliest fumes of off'rings consecrate.

I will not breathe save in your fragrant air,
Enlock me wholly in your shrine, accord
A single crumb from off your lavish board!
In sombre chasms this is now my prayer.

And HE: what meets my ear with stormy stir
Are wishes that inextricably vie,
With treasures craved by you, to gratify
Is not my office, honor I confer

Is not attained by force, this you shall know!
But then my arms against HIS knees I bowed,
With tongues of all my wakened yearning vowed:
Except you bless, I will not let you go.

In meinem leben rannen schlimme tage
Und manche töne hallten rauh und schrill.
Nun hält ein guter geist die rechte wage
Nun tu ich alles was der engel will.

Wenn auch noch oft an freudelosem ufer
Die seele bis zum schluchzen sich vergisst
Sie hört sogleich am ankerplatz den rufer:
Zu schönerm strand die segel aufgehisst!

Wenn mich aufs hohe meer geneigt ein neuer
Gewittersturm umtost vom wahne links
Vom tode rechts—so greift ER schnell das steuer
Der kräfte toben harrt des einen winks:

Gebietend schlichtet ER der wellen hader
Die wolken weichen reiner bläue dort . .
Bald zieht auf glatten wassern dein geschwader
Zur stillen insel zum gelobten port.

My life had sorry hours in its pale,
And many tones resounded harsh and shrill,
But now a Blesséd Spirit holds the scale,
Now I shall do in all the angel's will.

Though often still the soul on joyless coast
Forgets itself and weeps, without delay
It hears the crier at the anchor post:
Unfurl the sails! To fairer strands away!

When bent on brimming seas around me reel
New thunders of the tempest, right the Grave
And Madness left—HE swiftly grasps the wheel,
The raging forces wait upon his wave:

Imperiously HE calms the warring tide,
The clouds recede from limpid blue once more,
On quiet waters soon your fleet will glide
To tranquil islands, to the promised shore.

Du wirst nicht mehr die lauten fahrten preisen
Wo falsche flut gefährlich dich umstürmt
Und wo der abgrund schroffe felsen türmt
Um deren spitzen himmels adler kreisen.

In diesen einfachen gefilden lern
Den hauch der den zu kühlen frühling lindert
Und den begreifen der die schwüle mindert
Und ihrem kindesstammeln horche gern!

Du findest das geheimnis ewiger runen
In dieser halden strenger linienkunst
Nicht nur in mauermeeres zauberdunst.
'Schon lockt nicht mehr das Wunder der lagunen

Das allumworbene trümmergrosse Rom
Wie herber eichen duft und rebenblüten
Wie sie die Deines volkes hort behüten—
Wie Deine wogen—lebengrüner Strom!'

The sounding journeys you shall praise no more,
Where perilous and false the water leaps,
And where the chasm rears its rugged steeps
Around whose summits heaven's eagles soar.

Learn in these simple fields to apprehend
The breath that all-too frosty spring allays,
And that which renders less its sultry haze,
A willing ear their childish prattle lend!

You find the secret of eternal runes
Within these hills austerely drawn and pure,
Not only seas of stone with magic lure,
'No more the wonder beckons of lagoons,

Of great and ruined Rome, the world-wooed dream,
As vine and bitter scent of oaken grove,
As they who guard your people's treasure-trove:
Your waters, green with life, O surging stream!'

Uns die durch viele jahre zum triumfe
Des grossen lebens unsre lieder schufen
Ist es gebühr mit würde auch die dumpfe
Erinnrung an das dunkel vorzurufen:

Das haupt gebettet folgte noch in stummer
Ergebung alten ehren siegen straussen . .
Blumen der frühen heimat nickten draussen
Und luden schaukelnd ein zum langen schlummer.

Und jenes lezte schöne bild ist sachte
Zurückgesunken in der winde singen.
Kein freund war nahe mehr, sie alle gingen
Nur ER der niemals wankte blieb und wachte.

Mit der betäubung wein aus seinem sprengel
Die dichten schatten der bedrängnis hindernd
Des endes schwere scheideblicke lindernd
So stand am lager fest und hoch: der engel.

We, who for many years have made our songs
To praise Enchanted Life in all her might,
To us the fit and solemn task belongs
To fix the vague divinings of the night:

The pillowed head still mutely acquiesced
And followed ancient honors, gain and bout . . .
Flowers of early homeland stirred without
And rocking called to long and slumbrous rest.

And gently into winds of singing swayed
That image which is beautiful and last,
No friend remained beside, they all had passed,
But HE who never wavered, watched and stayed.

From aspergill with wine that deadens rue
The crowding shadows of oppression easing,
The heavy glances of the end appeasing,
The angel at the bed stood tall and true.

DER TEPPICH

Hier schlingen menschen mit gewächsen tieren
Sich fremd zum bund umrahmt von seidner franze
Und blaue sicheln weisse sterne zieren
Und queren sie in dem erstarrten tanze.

Und kahle linien ziehn in reich-gestickten
Und teil um teil ist wirr und gegenwendig
Und keiner ahnt das rätsel der verstrickten . .
Da eines abends wird das werk lebendig.

Da regen schauernd sich die toten äste
Die wesen eng von strich und kreis umspannet
Und treten klar vor die geknüpften quäste
Die lösung bringend über die ihr sannet!

Sie ist nach willen nicht: ist nicht für jede
Gewohne stunde: ist kein schatz der gilde.
Sie wird den vielen nie und nie durch rede
Sie wird den seltnen selten im gebilde.

THE TAPESTRY

Framed by a silken fringe, in strange accord
Here men are intermeshed with beasts and plants,
And sickles blue with stars of white are scored
And traverse them in the arrested dance.

Through lavish broideries run barren lines,
And part for part is tangled and at strife,
And none the riddle of the snared divines . . .
Then, on a night, the fabric comes to life.

Then frozen branches tremulously veer,
The beings close in line and circle fused
Emerge before the knotted tassels clear
And bring the answer over which you mused!

Not at your beck it is, and not for each
Accustomed hour, nor guild's enriching share,
And never for the many and through speech,
It comes incarnate rarely to the rare.

URLANDSCHAFT

Aus dunklen fichten flog ins blau der aar
Und drunten aus der lichtung trat ein paar
Von wölfen, schlürften an der flachen flut
Bewachten starr und trieben ihre brut.

Drauf huschte aus der glatten nadeln streu
Die schar der hinde trank und kehrte scheu
Zur waldnacht, eines blieb nur das im ried
Sein end erwartend still den rudel mied.

Hier litt das fette gras noch nie die schur
Doch lagen stämme, starker arme spur,
Denn drunten dehnte der gefurchte bruch
Wo in der scholle zeugendem geruch

Und in der weissen sonnen scharfem glühn
Des ackers froh des segens neuer mühn
Erzvater grub erzmutter molk
Das schicksal nährend für ein ganzes volk.

PRIMEVAL LANDSCAPE

From piny dark an eagle rose in air,
And from the clearing down below, a pair
Of wolves advanced and lapped the shallow flood,
Stood guard with rigid eyes and drove their brood.

Then hinds across the needles' glossy bed
In covies stole and drank and shyly fled
To wooded night, but in the marsh unstirred
Awaiting death was one who shunned the herd.

Here luscious grasses never felt the blade,
But stems—the work of sturdy arms—were laid,
And further down was spread the broken sod,
Where in the fertile odors of the clod

And in the white and stinging sun, content
With furrows, gains their novel labors spent,
First-mother milked, first-father hoed,
And so the fate of those to come, they sowed.

DER FREUND DER FLUREN

Kurz vor dem frührot sieht man in den fähren
Ihn schreiten, in der hand die blanke hippe
Und wägend greifen in die vollen ähren
Die gelben körner prüfend mit der lippe.

Dann sieht man zwischen reben ihn mit basten
Die losen binden an die starken schäfte
Die harten grünen herlinge betasten
Und brechen einer ranke überkräfte.

Er schüttelt dann ob er dem wetter trutze
Den jungen baum und misst der wolken schieben
Er gibt dem liebling einen pfahl zum schutze
Und lächelt ihm dem erste früchte trieben.

Er schöpft und giesst mit einem kürbisnapfe
Er beugt sich oft die quecken auszuharken
Und üppig blühen unter seinem stapfe
Und reifend schwellen um ihn die gemarken.

THE FRIEND OF THE FIELDS

One sees him walk the furrows through the gleaming
Of dawn, the shiny sickle in his grip,
And reach into the wheat to weigh its teeming,
He tests the yellow kernel with his lip.

Then on between the vines one sees him tying
With bast to sturdy prop, the shoots that strayed,
The grapes still hard and green with touches trying,
He prunes a tendril that too lushly swayed.

To see if it can brave the stormy weathers
He shakes the sapling, probes the drift of cloud,
To a support his favorite then he tethers
And smiles at one that first of fruits had bowed.

The water in a gourd he draws and showers,
He often bends to rake the quickening grasses,
And lavishly the region buds and flowers,
And ripens to the harvest where he passes.

DIE FREMDE

Sie kam allein aus fernen gauen
Ihr haus umging das volk mit grauen
Sie sott und buk und sagte wahr
Sie sang im mond mit offenem haar.

Am kirchtag trug sie bunten staat
Damit sie oft zur luke trat . .
Dann ward ihr lächeln süss und herb
Gatten und brüdern zum verderb.

Und übers jahr als sie im dunkel
Einst attich suchte und ranunkel
Da sah man wie sie sank im torf—
Und andere schwuren dass vorm dorf

Sie auf dem mitten weg verschwand . .
Sie liess das knäblein nur als pfand
So schwarz wie nacht so bleich wie lein
Das sie gebar im hornungschein.

THE STRANGER

She came alone from far away
Her house they skirted with dismay,
The palm she told and baked and stewed,
In moonlight sang without a snood.

Bedecked with gauds on holy day
Within her window oft she lay . . .
Then sweet and bitter grew her smile
To spouse and brother bane and guile.

The morrow-year when in the gloaming
For buttercup and elder roaming,
Some in the bog beheld her drown
But others swore beyond the town

Midways she disappeared and had
As only pledge bequeathed her lad,
As linen pale, as black as night,
Whom she had born in Feveril light.

DAS KLOSTER

Mit wenig brüdern flieht die lauten horden
Eh eure kraft verwelkt im kalten gift
Erbaut nach jungem wunsch das friedensstift
In einem stillen tal für euren orden.

Gewiegt von gleicher stunden mildem klang
Ist euch der keuschen erde arbeit heilig
Der tag verrinnt im wirken siebenteilig
Euch und der reinen schar die ich euch dang.

Umschlungen ohne lechzende begierde
Gefreundet ohne bangenden verdruss—
So flieht im abend schluchzen wort und kuss . .
Und solches ist der frommen paare zierde:

Von ebnem leid von ebner lust verzehrt
Zur blauen schönheit ihren blick zu richten
Geweihtes streben göttlichstes verzichten—
Wie einst ein mönch aus Fiesole gelehrt.

MONASTERY

From shouting mobs with few companions rally,
Before your strength in icy venom starve,
The church of peace, your early vision, carve,
To house your order in a silent valley.

By equal hours rocked in gentle toll,
Your labors in the virgin earth are praises,
The day of toil revolves in seven phases
For you, and those I gave you, chaste in soul.

In close embrace but far from craving passion,
As friends who never fret and never grieve—
Thus passes sobbing, word and kiss at eve . . .
And for the fervent pairs this motto fashion:

With even pain and even pleasure fraught
To lift their eyes to heaven-colored beauty,
Divine renouncing, consecrated duty—
As once a monk from Fiesole had taught.

JULI-SCHWERMUT

AN ERNEST DOWSON

Blumen des sommers duftet ihr noch so reich:
Ackerwinde im herben saatgeruch
Du ziehst mich nach am dorrenden geländer
Mir ward der stolzen gärten sesam fremd.

Aus dem vergessen lockst du träume: das kind
Auf keuscher scholle rastend des ährengefilds
In ernte-gluten neben nackten schnittern
Bei blanker sichel und versiegtem krug.

Schläfrig schaukelten wespen im mittagslied
Und ihm träufelten auf die gerötete stirn
Durch schwachen schutz der halme-schatten
Des mohnes blätter: breite tropfen blut.

Nichts was mir je war raubt die vergänglichkeit.
Schmachtend wie damals lieg ich in schmachtender
    flur
Aus mattem munde murmelt es: wie bin ich
Der blumen müd, der schönen blumen müd!

SADNESS IN JULY

TO ERNEST DOWSON

Flowers of summer, rich though your perfume be:
Meadow-tendrils in bitter scent of grain,
You draw me on along the withered paling,
Estranged to haughty gardens' sesame.

Out of oblivion, dreams you summon: the child
At rest on virgin earth in the acre of wheat,
In glows of harvest near the naked reapers,
With gleaming sickle and with empty jug.

Wasps were drowsily rocked in the song of noon,
Downward dripped on his forehead encrimsoned
    with sun,
Through slender screens of grassy shadows
The poppy petals: spreading drops of blood.

Nothing I ever owned can be filched by Time.
Thirsting as then in thirst-stricken fields I lie,
From fainting lips the murmur comes: how tired
I am of blooms, of lovely blooms, how tired!

MORGENSCHAUER

Lässt solch ein schmerz sich nieten
Und solch ein hauch und solch ein licht?
Der morgen sich gebieten
Der fremd und selig in uns bricht?

Wie durch die seele zogen
Die pfade—dann durch das gefild.
Gelinde düfte sogen
Dann gossen sie sich schnell und wild.

Trüb wie durch tränen schwimmen
Der baum, das haus das uns empfängt.
Ein weisses festtag-glimmen
Der kirschenzweig der überhängt

Ein rauschendes geflitter
Entzückt und quält—macht schwer und frei.
Ein schwanken süss und bitter
Ein singen sonder melodei . .

MORNING TREMOR

What rivets such a sorrow
And such a breath and such a flame?
What governs such a morrow
That blessed and strange upon us came?

Through fields the paths were shifted
As if they traced the soul's domain,
And fragile perfumes drifted,
Then wild and suddenly they rain.

Dim as through weeping, glimmer
The tree, the house that welcomes us.
A candid festal shimmer,
The cherry branch that hangs across,

A surging and a glitter,
Torment and charm—make grave and free,
A waver sweet and bitter,
A chanting without melody . . .

TAG-GESANG

Bewältigt vom rausche noch
   sah ich ihm nach
Er wandte sich dem der ihn
   liebend besprach.

Mein lob sich auf fittichen
   hin zu ihm schwang
Bis ganz ihn im westen
   die wolke umschlang.

Um wen soll ich werben mit
   minderem hall
Da nichts wie Er gross ist und
   nichts wie Er all!

So schritt ich vertrauert und
   horchte mit fleiss
Zu schluchten gebeugt auf ihr
   dunkles geheiss.

DAY-SONG

Enthralled still in rapture, my
    gaze toward him yearned,
To him who invoked with his
    love he was turned.

Across on its pinions my
    praise to him swung,
Till westerly clouds all
    about him were flung.

And whom shall I woo with
    more reverent call,
Since none great as He and since
    He only all!

So mournful I wandered and
    earnestly bent
Toward chasms to gather their
    sombre intent.

NACHT-GESANG

Mild und trüb
Ist mir fern
Saum und fahrt
Mein geschick.

Sturm und herbst
Mit dem tod
Glanz und mai
Mit dem glück.

Was ich tat
Was ich litt
Was ich sann
Was ich bin:

Wie ein brand
Der verraucht
Wie ein sang
Der verklingt.

NIGHT-SONG

Mild and dim
Lie afar
Stay and fare
Is my fate.

Storm and fall
With their death
Glow and May
With their joy.

What I thought
What I made
What I bore
What I am:

Like a flame
Gone in smoke
Like a song
Gone in wind.

TRAUM UND TOD

Glanz und ruhm! so erwacht unsre welt
Heldengleich bannen wir berg und belt
Jung und gross schaut der geist ohne vogt
Auf die flur auf die flut die umwogt.

Da am weg bricht ein schein fliegt ein bild
Und der rausch mit der qual schüttelt wild.
Der gebot weint und sinnt beugt sich gern
'Du mir heil du mir ruhm du mir stern'

Dann der traum höchster stolz steigt empor
Er bezwingt kühn den Gott der ihn kor . .
Bis ein ruf weit hinab uns verstösst
Uns so klein vor dem tod so entblösst!

All dies stürmt reisst und schlägt blizt und brennt
Eh für uns spät am nacht-firmament
Sich vereint schimmernd still licht-kleinod:
Glanz und ruhm rausch und qual traum und tod.

DREAM AND DEATH

Glow and fame! So our world turns to light,
Like the gods we subdue surge and height,
And the mind without lord, great and young,
Sees the field, sees the tide far outflung.

Vision flies, on the way shimmer breaks,
Frenzied bliss joined with pain, wildly shakes.
He who bade, thinks and weeps, bends in zeal,
'You my fame, you my star, you my weal!'

Now the dream, highest pride, upward springs,
Boldly quells then the god who lent wings . . .
Till a cry to the depth thrusts us all,
We so bare, faced with death, we so small!

All this gleamed, burned and stormed, struck and rent,
Till for us late in night-firmament
Calm and bright there is fused gem of flame:
Dream and death, bliss and pain, glow and fame.

FRANKEN

Es war am schlimmsten kreuzweg meiner fahrt:
Dort aus dem abgrund züngelnd giftige flammen,
Hier die gemiednen gaue wo der ekel
Mir schwoll vor allem was man pries und übte,
Ich ihrer und sie meiner götter lachten.
Wo ist dein dichter, arm und prahlend volk?
Nicht einer ist hier: Dieser lebt verwiesen
Und Jenem weht schon frost ums wirre haupt.

Da lud von Westen märchenruf . . so klang
Das lob des ahnen seiner ewig jungen
Grossmütigen erde deren ruhm ihn glühen
Und not auch fern ihn weinen liess, der mutter
Der fremden unerkannten und verjagten . .
Ein rauschen bot dem erben gruss als lockend
In freundlichkeit und fülle sich die ebnen
Der Maas und Marne unterm frühlicht dehnten.

Und in der heitren anmut stadt, der gärten
Wehmütigem reiz, bei nachtbestrahlten türmen
Verzauberten gewölbs umgab mich jugend
Im taumel aller dinge die mir teuer—
Da schirmten held und sänger das Geheimnis:
VILLIERS sich hoch genug für einen thron,
VERLAINE in fall und busse fromm und kindlich
Und für sein denkbild blutend: MALLARMÉ.

FRANKISH LANDS

Most evil was this forking of my ways:
There, from the chasm, tongues of baneful fire,
Here, regions to be shunned where loathing festered
In me for everything they praised and practiced.
I scoffed at their gods, mine they taunted! Where is
Your poet, poor and boastful people? None
Is here: for This One spends his days in exile,
And That One's frantic head is veiled in frost.

The West then called with fabled voice . . . so rang
The sire's praise of his forever lavish
Young land, whose glory thrilled, whose travail
        moved him
To tears, though he was distant, of the Mother
Of aliens, of the unesteemed and banished . . .
The heir was greeted by a surge when luring
In kindliness and plenitude, the basins
Of Meuse and Marne were spread beneath the sunrise.

And in the town of merry grace, in gardens
Of wistful charm, near nightly gleaming towers
With magic arches, youth was all about me
And swept away with all the things I cherish—
There bard and hero fended for the Secret:
VILLIERS who thought himself the peer of kings,
VERLAINE in fall and shrift devout and childlike,
And bleeding for his concept, MALLARMÉ.

Mag traum und ferne uns als speise stärken—
Luft die wir atmen bringt nur der Lebendige.
So dank ich freunde euch die dort noch singen
Und väter die ich seit zur gruft geleitet . . .
Wie oft noch spät da ich schon grund gewonnen
In trüber heimat streitend und des sieges
Noch ungewiss, lieh neue kraft dies flüstern:
RETURNENT FRANC EN FRANCE DULCE TERRE.

Though dream and distance give us strength and
    nurture—
Air that we breathe, the Living only proffer.
So friends who still are singing there, I thank you
And forebears that to graves I since have followed . . .
When I had gained a foothold—late—how often
As in my dreary land I strove, uncertain
Of victory, this whisper gave new vigors:
RETURNENT FRANC EN FRANCE DULCE TERRE.

LEO XIII

Heut da sich schranzen auf den thronen brüsten
Mit wechslermienen und unedlem klirren:
Dreht unser geist begierig nach verehrung
Und schauernd vor der wahren majestät
Zum ernsten väterlichen angesicht
Des Dreigekrönten wirklichen Gesalbten
Der hundertjährig von der ewigen burg
Hinabsieht: schatten schön erfüllten daseins.

Nach seinem sorgenwerk für alle welten
Freut ihn sein rebengarten: freundlich greifen
In volle trauben seine weissen hände,
Sein mahl ist brot und wein und leichte malve
Und seine schlummerlosen nächte füllt
Kein wahn der ehrsucht, denn er sinnt auf hymnen
An die holdselige Frau, der schöpfung wonne,
Und an ihr strahlendes allmächtiges kind.

'Komm heiliger knabe! hilf der welt die birst
Dass sie nicht elend falle! einziger retter!
In deinem schutze blühe mildre zeit
Die rein aus diesen freveln sich erhebe . .
Es kehre lang erwünschter friede heim
Und brüderliche bande schlinge liebe!'
So singt der dichter und der seher weiss:
Das neue heil kommt nur aus neuer liebe.

LEO XIII

Now that the thrones are held by brazen idlers,
With mien of brokers and with boastful rattle:
Our spirit avid to revere and trembling
Before the only actual majesty,
Turns to the grave paternal face of him,
The three-fold Crowned, the verily Anointed,
Who after life well lived a hundred years,
Peers as a shadow from his sacred stronghold.

When he has done the work for all his peoples,
The vineyard fills his leisure: heavy clusters
Of grapes his snowy fingers handle lightly.
His fare is bread and wine and weightless mallow,
And never are his sleepless midnights filled
With vain ambition, for on hymns he muses
For her, the world's delight: Our Blesséd Lady,
And for her radiant, her almighty Child.

'Come, Sainted Boy, and help the riven world,
Lest wretchedness destroy it, Sole Redeemer!
A gentler age shall bloom beneath your sign,
And rise untouched from all the desecrations . . .
May joys of long-desired peace return,
May Love bind each to each and make them brothers!'
So sings the poet and the prophet knows:
New love alone begets a new salvation.

Wenn angetan mit allen würdezeichen
Getragen mit dem baldachin—ein vorbild
Erhabnen prunks und göttlicher verwaltung—
Er eingehüllt von weihrauch und von lichtern
Dem ganzen erdball seinen segen spendet:
So sinken wir als gläubige zu boden
Verschmolzen mit der tausendköpfigen menge
Die schön wird wenn das wunder sie ergreift.

When all adorned with symbols of his office,
Uplifted with the baldachin—a pattern
Of lofty splendor and divine dominion—
Ensheathed in veils of incense and of candles,
To all the globe of earth he grants his blessings,
Then prostrate on the ground we sink: believers,
Who melt into the thousand-headed masses,
That moved with mystery, grow beautiful.

DAS ZEITGEDICHT

Ich euch gewissen, ich euch stimme dringe
Durch euren unmut der verwirft und flucht:
'Nur niedre herrschen noch, die edlen starben:
Verschwemmt ist glaube und verdorrt ist liebe.
Wie flüchten wir aus dem verwesten ball?'
Lasst euch die fackel halten wo verderben
Der zeit uns zehrt, wo ihr es schafft durch eigne
Erhizte sinne und zersplissnes herz.

Ihr wandet so das haupt bis ihr die Schönen
Die Grossen nicht mehr saht—um sie zu leugnen
Und stürztet ihre alt—und neuen bilder.
Ihr hobet über Körper weg und Boden
Aus rauch und staub und dunst den bau, schon wuchsen
In riesenformen mauern bogen türme—
Doch das gewölk das höher schwebte ahnte
Die stunde lang voraus wo er verfiel.

Dann krochet ihr in höhlen ein und riefet:
'Es ist kein tag. Nur wer den leib aus sich
Ertötet hat der lösung lohn: die dauer.'
So schmolzen ehmals blass und fiebernd sucher
Des golds ihr erz mit wässern in dem tiegel
Und draussen gingen viele sonnenwege . .
Da ihr aus gift und kot die seele kochtet
Verspriztet ihr der guten säfte rest.

A POEM OF MY TIMES

I am your conscience, I your voice pervading
Your malcontent that curses and condemns:
'The base alone still rule, the noble perished,
Belief is washed away and love is wilted.
How can we flee the foulness of the earth?'
Let torches show you where the era's ruin
Consumes you, where you shape it with the fevers
Of your own senses, with your ravelled heart.

You turned until you saw the Great no longer,
The Beautiful—in order to deny them,
And you dethroned their new, their ancient statues.
Beyond the Body and the Soil your structures
Of smoke and dust and fog you lifted, tower
And wall and arch began to grow gigantic—
But clouds that floated higher could have presaged
The hour long before when this would fall.

You crawled to caves: 'there is no day,' you
        clamored,
'And only he who killed the fleshly in
Himself is free and so he earns endurance.'
So seekers after gold once, pale and fevered,
Their ore in crucibles with tinctures melted,
And just without were many sunlit courses . . .
When you concocted souls from filth and poison
You spilled the residue of healthy saps.

Ich sah die nun jahrtausendalten augen
Der könige aus stein von unsren träumen
Von unsren tränen schwer . . sie wie wir wussten:
Mit wüsten wechseln gärten, frost mit glut,
Nacht kommt für helle—busse für das glück.
Und schlingt das dunkel uns und unsre trauer:
Eins das von je war—keiner kennt es—währet
Und blum und jugend lacht und sang erklingt.

I saw the Pharaohs gazing through millennia
With eyes of stone, by tears of ours burdened,
By dreams of ours weighed . . . as we, they also
Knew: deserts shift with gardens, frost with blaze,
Night comes for sun—atonement for delight.
And though despair and dark engulf us: One Thing
That ever was—none knows it—is eternal,
And youth and flowers laugh and songs resound.

Wenn dich meine wünsche umschwärmen
Mein leidender hauch dich umschwimmt—
Ein tasten und hungern und härmen:
So scheint es im tag der verglimmt
Als dränge ein rauher umschlinger
Den jugendlich biegsamen baum,
Als glitten erkaltete finger
Auf wangen von sonnigem flaum.

Doch schliessen die schatten sich dichter
So lenkt der gedanke dich zart.
Dann gelten die klänge und lichter,
Dann ist uns auf unserer fahrt:
Es schüttle die nacht ihre locken
Wo wirbel von sternen entfliegt,
Wir wären von klingenden flocken
Umglänzt und geführt und gewiegt.

Mich hoben die träume und mären
So hoch dass die schwere mir wich—
Dir brachten die träume die zähren
Um andre um dich und um mich . . .
Nun wird diese seele dir lieber
Die bleiche von duldungen wund,
Nun löscht sein verzehrendes fieber
Mein mund in dem blühenden mund.

When round you my wishes are thronging,
The breath of my suffering brims—
A groping, a starving and longing:
It seems in the day as it dims,
That harshly a lover is pressing
The tender young tree in embrace,
That fingers grown cold are caressing
A downy and radiant face.

But closer the shadows are leaning,
And thought has you gently in sway,
Then lustre and sounds gather meaning,
It seems to us then on our way,
That night shook her tresses and whirling
A shower of planets is fled,
That we by the flakes fallen purling
Are lighted and cradled and led.

By legends and dreams I was ravished
So high that from weight I am free.
The dreams on you weeping have lavished,
For others, for you and for me . . .
And more now this soul you desire,
Though pallid and wilted with drouth,
I calm my tempestous fire:
My mouth in the bloom of your mouth.

Trübe seele—so fragtest du—was trägst du trauer?
Ist dies für unser grosses glück dein dank?
Schwache seele—so sagt ich dir—schon ist in trauer
　　Dies glück verkehrt und macht mich sterbens
　　krank.

Bleiche seele—so fragtest du—dann losch die flamme
　　Auf ewig dir die göttlich in uns brennt?
Blinde seele—so sagt ich dir—ich bin voll flamme:
　　Mein ganzer schmerz ist sehnsucht nur die brennt.

Harte seele—so fragtest du—ist mehr zu geben
　　Als jugend gibt? ich gab mein ganzes gut . .
Und kann von höherem wunsch ein busen beben
　　Als diesem: nimm zu deinem heil mein blut!

Leichte seele—so sagt ich dir—was ist dir lieben!
　　Ein schatten kaum von dem was ich dir bot . .
Dunkle seele—so sagtest du—ich muss dich lieben
　　Ist auch durch dich mein schöner traum nun tot.

Soul in dimness—you asked of me—why are you
   mourning?
   Is this your thanks for all our great delight?
Soul in weakness—I said to you—already mourning
   All this delight became and deadly blight.

Soul in pallor—you asked of me—for you the fire
   Is wholly quenched, that godlike in us burns?
Soul in blindness—I said to you—I brim with fire:
   My sorrow's sum is only want that burns.

Soul in harshness—you asked of me—can more be given
   Than youth bestows? All that I have I cede . . .
And can a breast by nobler wish be riven
   Than this: that you may prosper, let me bleed!

Soul in lightness—I said to you—what is your loving!
   Of what I had for you—the merest shred . . .
Soul in darkness—you said to me—you chain my
   loving,
   Though now through you my shining dream
      is dead.

DANKSAGUNG

Die sommerwiese dürrt von arger flamme.
Auf einem uferpfad zertretnen kleees
Sah ich mein haupt umwirrt von zähem schlamme
Im fluss trübrot von ferner donner grimm.
Nach irren nächten sind die morgen schlimm:
Die teuren gärten wurden dumpfe pferche
Mit bäumen voll unzeitig giftigen schneees
Und hoffnungslosen tones stieg die lerche.

Da trittst du durch das land mit leichten sohlen
Und es wird hell von farben die du maltest.
Du lehrst vom frohen zweig die früchte holen
Und jagst den schatten der im dunkel kreucht . .
Wer wüsste je—du und dein still geleucht—
Bänd ich zum danke dir nicht diese krone:
Dass du mir tage mehr als sonne strahltest
Und abende als jede sternenzone.

GIVING THANKS

The summer field is parched with evil fire,
And from a shoreland trail of trodden clover
I saw my head in waters thick with mire
That wrath of far-off thunder dimmed with red.
The mornings after frantic nights are dread:
The cherished gardens turned to stifling stall,
Untimely snow of bane the trees filmed over,
And upward rose the lark with hopeless call.

Then through the land on weightless soles you stray,
And bright it grows with colors you have laid,
You bid us pluck the fruits from joyous spray,
And rout the shadows lurking in the night . . .
Did I not weave—you and your tranquil light—
This crown in thanks, who ever could have known
That more than sun, long days for me you rayed,
And evenings more than any starry zone.

Das lockere saatgefilde lechzet krank
Da es nach hartem froste schon die lauern
Lenzlichter fühlte und der pflüge zähne
Und vor dem stoss der vorjahr-stürme keuchte:
Sei mir nun fruchtend bad und linder trank
Von deiner nackten brust das blumige schauern
Das duften deiner leichtgewirrten strähne
Dein hauch dein weinen deines mundes feuchte.

The field of loosened earth is sick and craving
When after dour frost, already pressed
By warmer gleams of spring and harrow's share,
It heaves before the tempest's vernal sweeping:
Be now my draught of balm, my fertile laving
The bloomy tremor of your naked breast,
The fragrance of your softly tangled hair,
The moisture of your mouth, your breath, your
        weeping.

Da waren trümmer nicht noch scherben
Da war kein abgrund war kein grab
Da war kein sehnen war kein werben:
Wo eine stunde alles gab.

Von tausend blüten war ein quillen
Im purpurlicht der zauberei.
Des vogelsangs unbändig schrillen
Durchbrach des frühlings erster schrei.

Das war ein stürzen ohne zäume
Ein rasen das kein arm beengt—
Ein öffnen neuer duftiger räume
Ein rausch der alle sinne mengt.

There were no shards and no destruction,
There was no chasm and no pall,
There was no yearning, no seduction:
A single hour gave us all.

A thousand smiling blooms abounded
In crimson light of sorcery,
The primal cry of spring was sounded
In birdsong shrilling reinlessly.

There was a deluge with no holding,
A madness that no arm can stay—
A fragrant new-born space unfolding,
A reel that makes the senses sway.

Wieviel noch fehlte dass das fest sich jähre
Als schon aus einer gelben wolke frost
In spitzen körnern niederfiel! . . So sprosst
Denn keine unsrer saaten ohne zähre?

Für allen heftigen drang und zarten zwist‚
So gilt für alle lust die uns erhöhte
Für alle klagen und beweinten nöte
Der eine sonnenumlauf nur als frist.

Herüberhingen schwellend und geklärt
Die traubenbündel an den stöcken gestern‚
Die nun zu most der lang im dunkel gärt
Zerstossen werden und zu schaalen trestern.

Muss mit den ernten auch dies glück verfalben‚
Verlieren zier um zier mit halm und strauch
Und unaufhaltsam ziehen mit den schwalben‚
Verwehen spurlos mit dem sommerrauch?

How much was lacking still to round our year
Of festal days, when frost already spun
From yellow clouds in pointed grains! . . . Do none
Of all our seeds then bud without a tear?

For all of tender feud and ardor bold,
For all the joy that upward with us swept,
For all the plaints and sorrows we have wept,
A single circuit of the sun was doled.

The clustered grapes that yesterday had bent
The vines with luminous and swelling wreath,
To brews that in the darkness long ferment
Are trodden now, and to insipid sheath.

Must this delight as all the sheaves grow sallow,
With blade and bush bereft of grace for grace,
And fly irrevocably with the swallow,
Dissolve in summer haze without a trace?

LOBGESANG

Du bist mein herr! wenn du auf meinem weg,
Viel-wechselnder gestalt doch gleich erkennbar
Und schön, erscheinst beug ich vor dir den nacken.
Du trägst nicht waffe mehr noch kleid noch fittich
Nur Einen schmuck: ums haar den dichten kranz.
Du rührest an—ein duftiger taumeltrank
Befängt den sinn der deinen odem spürt
Und jede fiber zuckt von deinem schlag.
Der früher nur den Sänftiger dich hiess
Gedachte nicht dass deine rosige ferse
Dein schlanker finger so zermalmen könne.
Ich werfe duldend meinen leib zurück
Auch wenn du kommst mit deiner schar von tieren
Die mit den scharfen klauen mäler brennen
Mit ihren hauern wunden reissen, seufzer
Erpressend und unnennbares gestöhn.
Wie dir entströmt geruch von weicher frucht
Und saftigem grün: so ihnen dunst der wildnis.
Nicht widert staub und feuchte die sie führen,
Kein ding das webt in deinem kreis ist schnöd.
Du reinigst die befleckung, heilst die risse
Und wischst die tränen durch dein süsses wehn.
In fahr und fron, wenn wir nur überdauern,
Hat jeder tag mit einem sieg sein ende—
So auch dein dienst: erneute huldigung
Vergessnes lächeln ins gestirnte blau.

144

ENCOMIUM

You are my lord! When on my path you loom
In many changing shapes and yet familiar
And beautiful, I bend my neck before you.
No longer have you garments, wings or weapons,
You wear but one adornment: in your hair
The clustered wreath. You touch—a fragrant draught
Of frenzy sways the mind that feels your breath,
And every fibre quivers from your blow.
Who called you The Assuager in the past,
He never fancied that your slender finger
Your rosy heel could shatter so completely.
I fling my body back in patient pain,
Yes, even when you come with your battalions
Of beasts that brand a mark with pointed talons
And tear with fangs, extorting sighs and anguish
Unutterable. As from you is breathed
The scent of mellow fruit and sappy green,
From them the fetid odor of the jungle.
The wet and dust they reek does not repel us:
No thing that in your circle weaves is foul.
You cleanse the taint, you heal the gash and banish
All weeping with the sweetness you exhale.
In threat or thrall, if only we are steadfast
Each day shall have in victory its ending—
Your service also: homage done again,
Oblivious smile into the starry blue.

TRAUER

Weh ruft vom walde.
Er schmückte sich mit frischem laub umsonst.
Die flur erharrte dich dass du sie weihtest.
Sie friert da du sie nun nicht sonnst:
Die zarten halme zittern an der halde
Die du nun nie beschreitest.

Was sind die knospen all die du nicht weckst,
Die äste all die deine hand nicht flicht,
Was sind die blumen all die sie nicht bricht,
Was sollen früchte sein die du nicht schmeckst!

Im jungen schlag ein krachen
Von stamm nach stamm—wann fällt der nächste?
Das morgendliche grün erschlafft.
Das kaum entsprossne gras liegt hingerafft.
Kein vogel singt . . nur frostiger winde lachen
Und dann der schall der äxte.

SORROW

Woods cry in anguish.
In vain they decked themselves in leaves of spring,
The field awaited you to bless it, numb
With cold, since now no sun you bring:
The fragile grasses on the hillside languish
Where now you never come.

What are the buddings that you do not wake,
The branches that your fingers do not weave,
What are the flowers that you do not reave,
The fruits you do not taste—whom shall they slake!

In sappy timber cracking
Of stem for stem—what next is bowed?
The morning green is growing worn,
The blades scarce risen upward, lying shorn,
No bird sings . . . only frosty winds are clacking,
And then the axe is loud.

AUF DAS LEBEN

UND DEN TOD MAXIMINS

Ihr hattet augen trüb durch ferne träume
Und sorgtet nicht mehr um das heilige lehn.
Ihr fühltet endes-hauch durch alle räume—
Nun hebt das haupt! denn euch ist heil geschehn.

In eurem schleppenden und kalten jahre
Brach nun ein frühling neuer wunder aus,
Mit blumiger hand, mit schimmer um die haare
Erschien ein gott und trat zu euch ins haus.

Vereint euch froh da ihr nicht mehr beklommen
Vor lang verwichner pracht erröten müsst:
Auch ihr habt eines gottes ruf vernommen
Und eines gottes mund hat euch geküsst.

Nun klagt nicht mehr—denn auch ihr wart erkoren—
Dass eure tage unerfüllt entschwebt . . .
Preist eure stadt die einen gott geboren!
Preist eure zeit in der ein gott gelebt!

ON THE LIFE

AND DEATH OF MAXIMIN

Your eyes were dim with distant dreams, you tended
No more with care the holy fief and knew
In every space the breath of living ended—
Now lift your head for joy has come to you.

The cold and dragging year that was your share,
A vernal tide of dawning wonders bore,
With bloomy hand, with shimmers in his hair
A god appeared and stepped within your door.

Unite in gladness, now no longer darkened
And flushing for an age whose gold is flown:
The calling of a god you too have hearkened,
It was a god whose mouth has kissed your own.

You also were elect—no longer mourn
For all your days in unfulfillment sheathed . . .
Praise to your city where a god was born!
Praise to your age in which a god has breathed!

BESUCH

Sanftere sonne fällt schräg
Durch deiner mauer scharten
In deinen kleinen garten
Und dein haus am gehäg.

Schwirren die vögel im plan,
Regen sträuche die ruten:
Ziehen nach tagesgluten
Erste wandrer die bahn.

Fülle die eimer nun strack!
Netze im pfade die kiese
Büsche und beete der wiese
Häng-ros und güldenlack!

Und bei der wand am gestühl
Brich den zu wirren eppich!
Streue blumen zum teppich!
Duftend sei es und kühl

VISIT

Sun with a mellower fall
Plot of your garden edges,
Slants through the house in hedges
Down through gaps in the wall.

Birds are astir on the grass,
Twigs of bushes are blowing,
After the daystar's glowing
Farers now again pass.

Fill then the bucket straightway!
Shower the gravel and osiers,
Flowers unfolding in closures,
Wall-bloom and rose asway!

And near the bricks by the seat,
Break the ivy too lavish!
Buds for a carpet ravish!
Cool be the air and sweet

Wenn ER als pilgersmann
In solchen dämmerungen
Nochmals vielleicht durchdrungen
Unsere erde und dann

Ueberm weg das geäst
Teilt mit dem heiligen oden—
Er eine weil deinen boden
Tritt und sich niederlässt!

In such a twilight when
HE as a pilgrim paces
Once more perhaps the places
On our earth here, and then

Branches hung on the way
Boon of his breath has divided—
Over your garden he glided,
Enters and wants to stay!

ENTRUECKUNG

Ich fühle luft von anderem planeten.
Mir blassen durch das dunkel die gesichter
Die freundlich eben noch sich zu mir drehten.

Und bäum und wege die ich liebte fahlen
Dass ich sie kaum mehr kenne und Du lichter
Geliebter schatten—rufer meiner qualen—

Bist nun erloschen ganz in tiefern gluten
Um nach dem taumel streitenden getobes
Mit einem frommen schauer anzumuten.

Ich löse mich in tönen, kreisend, webend,
Ungründigen danks und unbenamten lobes
Dem grossen atem wunschlos mich ergebend.

Mich überfährt ein ungestümes wehen
Im rausch der weihe wo inbrünstige schreie
In staub geworfner beterinnen flehen.

TRANSPORT

I feel an air from other planets flowing,
In darkness faces pale upon my sight
That even now had turned on me their glowing.

And trees and paths I loved in greyness languish,
So that I hardly know them, and your light,
Belovéd shadow—bidder of my anguish—

In deeper blazes now is wholly blended
To touch with blest and tremulous amaze,
When frenzy of chaotic strife is ended.

In music I am melted, circling, wreathing,
Of thanks unfathomed and unbounded praise,
Surrendered wishless to the mighty breathing.

Now I am shaken as with tempest soaring
In sacred rapture where with frantic screams
The fervent sink into the dust, imploring.

Dann seh ich wie sich duftige nebel lüpfen
In einer sonnerfüllten klaren freie
Die nur umfängt auf fernsten bergesschlüpfen.

Der boden schüttert weiss und weich wie molke . .
Ich steige über schluchten ungeheuer,
Ich fühle wie ich über lezter wolke

In einem meer kristallnen glanzes schwimme—
Ich bin ein funke nur vom heiligen feuer
Ich bin ein dröhnen nur der heiligen stimme.

Then I behold how bloomy mist disperses
In limpid space suffused with sunny beams,
That only on the furthest peaks immerses.

As soft and white as whey the ground is shifted . . .
Across enormous chasms high and higher,
I feel how over last of clouds uplifted

In seas of crystal radiance I am swung—
I only am a spark of holy fire,
A thunder only of the holy tongue!

URSPRUENGE

Heil diesem lachenden zug:
Herrlichsten gutes verweser
Maasslosen glückes erleser!
Schaltend mit göttlichem fug
Traget ihr kronen und psalter.
Später gedenkt es euch kaum:
Nie lag die welt so bezwungen,
Eines geistes durchdrungen
Wie im jugend-traum.

Heil dir sonnenfroh gefild
Wo nach sieg der heiligen rebe
Nach gefälltem wald und wild
Kam in kränzen Pan mit Hebe!
Rauhe jäger zottige rüden
Wichen weissem marmorbein.
Hallen luden wie im süden . .
Wir empfingen noch den schein.
Aus den aufgewühlten gruben
Dampfte odem von legion
Und von trosses fraun und buben,
Hier ihr gold ihr erz ihr thon!
Auf dem bergweg seht die schaar—
Eine stampfende kohorte!
Offen stehen brück und pforte
Für des Caesarsohnes aar.

ORIGINS

Hail to this laughing array:
Regent of sumptuous treasure
Chosen for gifts without measure!
Ruling with heavenly sway,
Circlets you carry and psalters.
Later to none it will seem
That once the world was so captured,
By One spirit enraptured,
As in youth with dream.

Hail O meadow blessed with sun
Where when holy grapes were pressed,
Came—the deer and forest done—
Pan and Hebe blossom dressed.
Rugged hunter, shaggy hound,
Cede to limbs of marble shimmer,
Halls by Rome's proportion bound . . .
We were granted still a glimmer.
From the pits then open laid,
Breath of legions upward rolled,
Women, boys in cavalcade,
Here their clay, their ore, their gold!
See the host on mountain ridge—
Cohorts tread in rhythms regal!
For the Caesar scion's eagle
Wide the portal and the bridge.

Auf diesen trümmern hob die Kirche dann ihr haupt,
Die freien nackten leiber hat sie streng gestaupt,
Doch erbte sie die prächte die nur starrend schliefen
Und übergab das maass der höhen und der tiefen
Dem sinn der beim hosiannah über wolken blieb
Und dann zerknirscht sich an den gräberplatten rieb.

Doch an dem flusse im schilfpalaste
Trieb uns der wollust erhabenster schwall:
In einem sange den keiner erfasste
Waren wir heischer und herrscher vom All.
Süss und befeuernd wie Attikas choros
Ueber die hügel und inseln klang:
Co besoso pasoje ptoros
Co es on hama pasoje boañ.

Above these ruins then, the Churches' head emerged,
The bodies free and bare, with bitterness she scourged,
But she was heir to pomp that only stared while sleep-
    ing,
And measure set for heights and depths, she gave in
    keeping
To minds that in Hosannas towered over cloud,
And then on slabs of graves in self-abasement bowed.

But near the stream in a palace of reed,
On by the tide of our lust we were swirled,
Singing an anthem that no one could read,
We were the masters and lords of the world.
Sweet and inciting as Attica's chorus
Over the hills and the islands flung:
Co besoso pasoje ptoros
Co es on hama pasoje boañ.

LANDSCHAFT

Des jahres wilde glorie durchläuft
Der trübe sinn der mittags sich verlor
In einem walde wo aus spätem flor
Von safran rost und purpur leiden träuft.

Und blatt um blatt in breiten flecken fällt
Auf schwarze glätte eines trägen bronns
Wo schon des dunkels grausamer gespons
Ein knabe kühlen auges wache hält . .

Und durch die einsamkeiten stumm und taub
Senkt langsam flammend sich von ast zu ast
Ins schwere gelb des abends goldner glast—
Dann legt sich finstrer dunst in finstres laub.

Nachtschatten ranken, flaumiges gebräm,
Um einen wall von nacktem blutigen dorn,
Gerizte hände dringen matt nach vorn . .
Dass in das dickicht nun der schlummer käm! . .

LANDSCAPE

Across the year's untrammelled glory slips
The listless spirit lost at noonday hour,
Within a wood where from the tardy flower
Of saffron, rust and purple, sorrow drips.

And leaf for leaf in ample patches sweeps
Across a sombre, smooth and languid pool,
Where even now a boy whose eyes are cool,
The ruthless spouse of dark, the vigil keeps . . .

And through the deaf and soundless solitudes,
From branch to branch descends aflame and slow
To heavy yellow, evening's golden glow—
Then brooding leaves are filmed with mist that broods.

The nightshade clambers as a downy edge
Around a wall of bare and bleeding thorn,
And wearied hands are forward thrust and torn . . .
If only slumber came into the sedge! . . .

Da bricht durch wirres grau ein blinken scheu
Und neue helle kommt aus dämmerung.
Ein anger dehnt auf einem felsensprung
Weithin . . nur zieht durch der violen streu

Die reihe schlanker stämme, speer an speer,
Von silber flimmert das gewölbte blau,
Ein feuchter wind erhebt sich duftend lau . . .
Es fallen blüten auf ein offen meer.

Then timid gleams the grey confusion rend,
And new resplendence from the dusk is shed,
A meadow on a jutting cliff is spread
Far off . . . through strewn violas only wend

The rows of slender lances: tree for tree,
A silver glamor fills the vaulted blue,
A fragrant wind awakes of warmth and dew . . .
And blossoms fall upon an open sea.

LITANEI

Tief ist die trauer
                        die mich umdüstert,
Ein tret ich wieder
                        Herr! in dein haus . .

Lang war die reise,
                        matt sind die glieder,
Leer sind die schreine,
                        voll nur die qual.

Durstende zunge
                        darbt nach dem weine.
Hart war gestritten,
                        starr ist mein arm.

Gönne die ruhe
                        schwankenden schritten,
Hungrigem gaume
                        bröckle dein brot!

Schwach ist mein atem
                        rufend dem traume,
Hohl sind die hände,
                        fiebernd der mund . .

LITANY

Deep is the sorrow
               darkened around me,
Lord! I repair to
               house that is yours . . .

Limbs are exhausted
               much did I fare through,
Empty the altars
               full only grief.

Tongue for the vintage
               thirstily falters,
Hard I contended
               numb is my arm.

Tottering footsteps
               respite be lended,
Palate unsated
               portion your bread!

Calling to vision
               breath now is bated,
Palms lifted hollow,
               fevered the mouth . . .

Leih deine kühle,
                    lösche die brände,
Tilge das hoffen,
                    sende das licht!

Gluten im herzen
                    lodern noch offen,
Innerst im grunde
                    wacht noch ein schrei . .

Töte das sehnen,
                    schliesse die wunde!
Nimm mir die liebe,
                    gieb mir dein glück!

Quench conflagration
           coolness shall follow,
Hoping be ended,
           vouchsafe the light!

Heart in its fires
           glows still unspended,
Cry still I cherish
           deep in my core . . .

Whole be the wounded,
           yearning shall perish!
Ease me of passion,
           give me your joy!

HEHRE HARFE

Sucht ihr neben noch das übel
Greift ihr aussen nach dem heile:
Giesst ihr noch in lecke kübel,
Müht ihr euch noch um das feile.

Alles seid ihr selbst und drinne:
Des gebets entzückter laut
Schmilzt in eins mit jeder minne,
Nennt sie Gott und freund und braut!

Keine zeiten können borgen . .
Fegt der sturm die erde sauber:
Tretet ihr in euren morgen,
Werfet euren blick voll zauber

Auf die euch verliehnen gaue
Auf das volk das euch umfahet
Und das land das dämmergraue
Das ihr früh im brunnen sahet.

Hegt den wahn nicht: mehr zu lernen
Als aus staunen überschwang
Holden blumen hohen sternen
EINEN sonnigen lobgesang.

SACRED LYRE

Outward ills you still are seeking?
Grasp for joys beyond your pale?
Fill the buckets that are leaking?
Still you strive to what's for sale?

You are all and all you fashion:
Prayers in enchanted tide,
Melt to one with every passion
Call it God or friend or bride!

Never can an era borrow . . .
When the earth has felt the blast,
You shall enter on your morrow,
Glances bright with magic cast

On the throng around you surging,
On your own allotted field,
On your realm from dusk emerging
That a bourn had once revealed.

Cherish not the dream of knowing
More from wonder, sunward flight,
Circling planets, flowers blowing
Than a paean full of light.

LIEDER

Dies ist ein lied
Für dich allein:
Von kindischem wähnen
Von frommen tränen . .
Durch morgengärten klingt es
Ein leichtbeschwingtes.
Nur dir allein
Möcht es ein lied
Das rühre sein.

An baches ranft
Die einzigen frühen
Die hasel blühen.
Ein vogel pfeift
In kühler au.
Ein leuchten streift
Erwärmt uns sanft
Und zuckt und bleicht.
Das feld ist brach,
Der baum noch grau . .
Blumen streut vielleicht
Der lenz uns nach.

SONGS

This is a song
For none but you:
A childish ditty,
A tear of pity . . .
Through garden-morns it quavers
And lightly wavers.
For none but you,
Be it a song
That renders rue.

Beside the stream
The very first,
The hazels burst.
Bird-whistled notes
On frosty way,
Around us floats
And warms a gleam
With pallid thrill.
The fallow looms,
The tree still grey,
But the spring may fill
Our tracks with blooms.

LIEDER

Im morgen-taun
Trittst du hervor
Den kirschenflor
Mit mir zu schaun,
Duft einzuziehn
Des rasenbeetes.
Fern fliegt der staub . .
Durch die natur
Noch nichts gediehn
Von frucht und laub—
Rings blüte nur . .
Von süden weht es.

Kreuz der strasse . .
Wir sind am end.
Abend sank schon . .
Dies ist das end.
Kurzes wallen
Wen macht es müd?
Mir zu lang schon . .
Der schmerz macht müd.
Hände lockten:
Was nahmst du nicht?
Seufzer stockten:
Vernahmst du nicht?
Meine strasse
Du ziehst sie nicht.
Tränen fallen
Du siehst sie nicht.

SONGS

You came to view
The cherry tree
In bud, with me
In morning dew.
We drink the scent
Of grassy rows,
Dust far is swirled . . .
No leaves are sprung,
No fruit is spent
In Nature's world—
Just blooms are flung . . .
And southwind blows.

Fork of pathways . . .
We reached the end.
Shadows throng now . . .
This is the end.
Brief the going,
Whom does it tire?
All too long now . . .
And sorrows tire!
Hands are waiting:
Then why not clasp?
Sobs abating:
You do not grasp?
On my pathway
You do not fare,
Tears are flowing,
You do not care!

Mein kind kam heim.
Ihm weht der seewind noch im haar,
Noch wiegt sein tritt
Bestandne furcht und junge lust der fahrt.

Vom salzigen sprühn
Entflammt noch seiner wange brauner schmelz:
Frucht schnell gereift
In fremder sonnen wildem duft und brand.

Sein blick ist schwer
Schon vom geheimnis das ich niemals weiss
Und leicht umflort
Da er vom lenz in unsern winter traf.

So offen quoll
Die knospe auf dass ich fast scheu sie sah
Und mir verbot
Den mund der einen mund zum kuss schon kor.

Mein arm umschliesst
Was unbewegt von mir zu andrer welt
Erblüht und wuchs—
Mein eigentum und mir unendlich fern.

My child came home
The sea-wind tangled in his hair,
His gait still rocks
With conquered fears and young desire for quest.

The salty spray
Still tans and burns the bloom upon his cheek:
Fruit swiftly ripe
In savage scent and flame of alien suns.

His eyes are grave
With secrets now, that I shall never learn,
And faintly veiled,
Since from a spring he came into our frost.

So wide the bud
That almost shyly I withdrew my gaze,
And I abstained
From lips that had already chosen lips.

My arm enclasps
One who unmoved by me, grew up and bloomed
To other worlds—
My own and yet, how very far from me!

Hier ist nicht mein lichtrevier
Wo ich herrschte wo ich freite.
Himmel ist mir fremd und breite—
Arme flur mit magrer zier.

Sandige strecken unbebaut . .
Zwischen halden die verdorren
Streckt die dünnbelaubten knorren
Hier ein baum aus hagrem kraut.

Welch ein zirpen dringt ans ohr?
Vom gezweig ein tönend wispeln . .
Nun erkenn ich Dich am lispeln.
Du bist nah: bald scheinst du vor!

Nirgends weiss ich ziel und steg
Wem zu freude wem zu nutze
Und ich weiss mich nur im schutze:
Bin auch hier auf Deinem weg.

This is not my light-domain
Where I reigned and where I wooed,
Strange are skies and latitude—
Meagre growth on fallow plain.

Sandy stretches bare of seed . . .
Here between the slopes that parch
Trees with scanty foliage arch
Knotted in the puny weed.

What a chirping meets my ear?
Murmurs whisper from the bough . . .
By your voice I guess you now.
I shall see you: You are near!

Nowhere goal or path I know,
Joy to whom, to whom a yield?
This alone must be my shield:
Everywhere Your way I go.

NORDISCHER MEISTER

Wo dein geheimnis lag und dein gebreste
War unsrer nächte quälender vertreib:
Du malst in deine himmel ein die reste
Von glanz um der gefallnen engel leib.

JAHRHUNDERTSPRUCH

Auch ihr gabt euer erbteil fur ein mus . .
Bald gilt euch köstlicher erwerb für plunder,
Ihr nehmt als wahrheit nur die tollsten wunder . . .
Weh! was bricht los und rennt mit nacktem fuss!

VERFUEHRER

Wir sind nicht voll, wir haben nicht die drei
Und möchten doppelt sein mit unsrer zwei.
So rufen flehend wir die vier herbei
Aus nebel wahn und spuk und hexerei.

NORTHERN PAINTER

Wherein your secrets and your weakness lie
We spent our nights in torment, to discover:
You paint the shreds of glow into your sky
That round the limbs of fallen angels hover.

CENTENARY LINES

You also for a pottage gave your dole . . .
Soon precious gains from trash you cannot sunder,
Nothing for truth you take but maddest wonder . . .
What's loose, alas! and runs on naked sole!

TEMPTER

Our sum is not complete, we lack the thrice,
And would be rendered double with our twice.
So we invoke the four imploringly
From fog, from madness, spook and witchery.

DU STETS NOCH ANFANG UNS UND END UND MITTE
Auf deine bahn hienieden, Herre der Wende,
Dringt unser preis hinan zu deinem sterne.
Damals lag weites dunkel überm land
Der tempel wankte und des Innern flamme
Schlug nicht mehr hoch uns noch von andrem fiebern
Erschlafft als dem der väter: nach der Heitren
Der Starken Leichten unerreichten thronen
Wo bestes blut uns sog die sucht der ferne . . .
Da kamst du spross aus unsrem eignen stamm
Schön wie kein bild und greifbar wie kein traum
Im nackten glanz des gottes uns entgegen:
Da troff erfüllung aus geweihten händen
Da ward es licht und alles sehnen schwieg.

You, ALWAYS OUR BEGINNING, END AND MIDDLE
Our song of praise on your terrestrial farings
Now rises to your star, O Lord of Turning!
We felt a darkness laid across the land,
The temple tottered and the inner fires
No longer leaped for us, whom other fevers
Had wasted than our fathers': toward the joyful,
The strong, the poised, on thrones unreached, that
    squandered
Our noblest blood in lust for far horizons . . .
Then you, our own, from native stock appeared,
Confronting us in naked glows of godhood:
No statue was so fair, no dream so real!
Then out of hallowed hands fulfillment flooded,
Then there was light and every yearning stilled.

War wieder zeiten-fülle? Welche glut
'Als wollte eine welt sich neu gebären?'
Hell-lichte mittage wo schemen liefen . .
Die nächte mit dem tanz um offne feuer . .
Die roten fackelhalter und die weissen
Kranz-trägerinnen . . geller ton der pfeifen
Und aller einung im gemischten kuss.
Dann wenn es dämmerte griff uns der geist
Von ihm besessen quoll im wechsel rede
Entzückte uns zu schwur und todesweihe
Bis jeder lezte schauer bat: o komme
Du halt du klang in unsren tollen wirbeln
Du unsrer feier heiligung und krone
In unsrem dunklen träumen du der strahl!

Was Time again at zenith? What a glow,
'As though a world anew would be engendered?'
Clear radiance of noon when spectres flitted,
The nights with dances round the open fires,
The ruddy boys with torches and the candid
Girls bearing garlands . . . flutes resounding shrilly
And all in mingled kisses interfused.
Then with the dawn the spirit captured us,
Beneath its frenzy flooded word and answer,
Enchanted us to plighting faith and death-vows,
Till every final tremor pled: O hasten,
You song, you pillar in our curbless whirling,
You crown and consecration of our revels,
Within our dreaming darkness, you the beam!

Ich bin der Eine und bin Beide
Ich bin der zeuger bin der schooss
Ich bin der degen und die scheide
Ich bin das opfer bin der stoss
Ich bin die sicht und bin der seher
Ich bin der bogen bin der bolz
Ich bin der altar und der fleher
Ich bin das feuer und das holz
Ich bin der reiche bin der bare
Ich bin das zeichen bin der sinn
Ich bin der schatten bin der wahre
Ich bin ein end und ein beginn.

I am the One and am the Twain.
I am the womb I am the sire
I am the blow and am the slain
I am the wood I am the fire
I am the seer I am the sight
I am the sheath and am the haft
I am the shadow and the right
I am the bow I am the shaft
I am the rich I am the needer
I am the semblance and the heart
I am the altar and the pleader
I am a finish and a start.

Alles habend alles wissend seufzen sie:
'Karges leben! drang und hunger überall!
Fülle fehlt!'

Speicher weiss ich über jedem haus
Voll von korn das fliegt und neu sich häuft—
Keiner nimmt . .

Keller unter jedem hof wo siegt
Und im sand verströmt der edelwein—
Keiner trinkt . .

Tonnen puren golds verstreut im staub:
Volk in lumpen streift es mit dem saum—
Keiner sieht.

All possessing, all enlightened they deplore:
'Life is meagre! Urge and hunger everywhere!
Want of fill!'

Lofts I know on top of every house,
Full of grain that flies and teems anew—
No one takes . . .

Cellars under every hall where wines
Dry and stream away into the sand—
No one drinks . . .

Tons of purest gold dispersed in dust:
Men in tatters brush it with their hems—
No one sees.

Die ihr die wilden dunklen zeiten nennt
In eurer lughaft freien milden klugen:
Sie wollten doch durch grausen marter mord
Durch fratze wahn und irrtum hin zum gott.
Ihr frevler als die ersten tilgt den gott
Schafft einen götzen nicht nach Seinem bild
Kosend benamt und greulich wie noch keiner
Und werft ihm euer bestes in den schlund.
Ihr nennt es EUREN weg und wollt nicht ruhn
In trocknem taumel rennend bis euch allen
Gleich feig und feil statt Gottes rotem blut
Des götzen eiter in den adern rinnt.

What you have termed the dark and savage age
In days that boast of freedom, knowledge, mercy:
That strove at least through torture, murder, dread,
Through grimace, error, madness, on to god.
You felons are the first to down the god,
Carve out an idol not resembling Him,
Hailed by sweet names and gruesome as no other,
And hurl the best you have into its jaws.
You call it YOUR approach and will not rest
In torrid frenzy running, till all venal
And base alike, instead of God's red blood,
The pus of idols courses through your veins.

Auf stiller stadt lag fern ein blutiger streif.
Da zog vom dunkel über mir ein wetter
Und zwischen seinen stössen hört ich schritte
Von scharen, dumpf, dann nah. Ein eisern klirren . .
Und jubelnd drohend klang ein dreigeteilter
Metallen heller ruf und wut und kraft
Und schauer überfielen mich als legte
Sich eine flache klinge mir aufs haupt—
Ein schleunig pochen trieb zum trab der rotten . .
Und immer weitere scharen und derselbe
Gelle fanfaren-ton . . . Ist das der lezte
Aufruhr der götter über diesem land?

Above the silent town a streak of blood!
Then from the darkness over us, a tempest
Arose and through its gusts I heard a tramping
Of armies, dim then near. An iron clatter . . .
And joyful, threatening rang a thrice-divided
Metallic high-resounding call, and rage
And force and tremor over me were loosened,
As if a sword sank flat upon my head—
A rapid rhythm drove the troops to trotting . . .
And more and more battalions and the selfsame
Stridor of fanfare-tone . . . is this the final
Uprising of the gods above this land?

Einer stand auf der scharf wie blitz und stahl
Die klüfte aufriss und die lager schied
Ein Drüben schuf durch umkehr eures Hier . .
Der euren wahnsinn so lang in euch schrie
Mit solcher wucht dass ihm die kehle barst.
Und ihr? ob dumpf ob klug ob falsch ob echt
Vernahmt und saht als wäre nichts geschehn . .
Ihr handelt weiter sprecht und lacht und heckt.
Der warner ging . . dem rad das niederrollt
Zur leere greift kein arm mehr in die speiche.

One there emerged who sharp as flash and steel
Revealed the chasms and divided camps,
A Yonder wrought, reversing Here of yours . . .
Who cried your madness into you so long,
With such insistence that his throat was cracked.
And you? If dull, if shrewd, if false, if true,
You heard and saw as though no change had come,
Continued acting, talking, laughing, mating.
The Warner passed . . . no other arm will stop
The wheel that down to emptiness is driven.

Weltabend lohte . . wieder ging der Herr
Hinein zur reichen stadt mit tor und tempel
Er arm verlacht der all dies stürzen wird.
Er wusste: kein gefügter stein darf stehn
Wenn nicht der grund, das ganze, sinken soll.
Die sich bestritten nach dem gleichen trachtend:
Unzahl von händen rührte sich und unzahl
Gewichtiger worte fiel und Eins war not.
Weltabend lohte . . rings war spiel und sang
Sie alle sahen rechts—nur Er sah links.

World-evening glowed . . . again the Lord is come
To gate and temple of the sumptuous city,
He, poor and mocked, who all of this will raze.
He knows: no mortared stone may keep its place,
Lest the foundations everywhere collapse.
Those who were still at odds though like in striving:
Countless the hands that moved about and countless
Big words that fell and needed was but One.
World-evening glowed . . . and all was play and song,
They all were looking right—but He looked left.

Ihr Aeusserste von windumsauster klippe
Und schneeiger brache! Ihr von glühender wüste!
Stammort des gott-gespenstes . . gleich entfernte
Von heitrem meer und Binnen wo sich leben
Zu ende lebt in welt von gott und bild! . .
Blond oder schwarz demselben schooss entsprungne
Verkannte brüder suchend euch und hassend
Ihr immer schweifend und drum nie erfüllt!

You uttermost from wind-encompassed boulders,
And snowy fallows! You from glowing deserts,
Home of the spectral God, are just as distant
From buoyant sea and inland, where existence
Is ringed by worlds of image and of God! . . .
You, dark or blond, the selfsame womb begot you,
Each seeks and hates and does not know his brother,
Forever roams and never is fulfilled.

Fragbar ward Alles da das Eine floh:
Der geist entwand sich blindlings aus der siele
Entlaufne seele ward zum törigen spiele—
Sagbar ward Alles: drusch auf leeres stroh.
Nun löst das herz von wut und wahn verschlackt
Von gärung dunkelheit gespinst und trubel:
Die Tat ist aufgerauscht in irdischem jubel
Das Bild erhebt im licht sich frei und nackt.

All can be doubted since the One evades:
The spirit blindly struggled from the yoke
The truant soul became an idle joke—
All can be shouted: thresh on empty blades.
From ferment, tumult, chrysalis and night
Now loose the heart in rage and madness merged:
The Deed in earthly joy has upward surged,
The Image free and naked rears in light.

BREIT' IN DER STILLE DEN GEIST
Unter dem reinen gewölk
Send ihn zu horchender ruh
Lang in die furchtbare nacht
Dass er sich reinigt und stärkt
Du dich der hüllen befreist
Du nicht mehr stumm bist und taub
Wenn sich der gott in dir regt
Wenn dein geliebter dir raunt.

SPREAD IN THE STILLNESS YOUR MIND
Under immaculate cloud,
Long into terrors of night,
Send it to listen and rest
That it be strengthened and cleansed,
You of your sheath rendered free,
You no more silent and deaf
When you are moved by the god,
When your Beloved to you breathes.

Was gelitten ist beschwichte!
Widergeist ist nun bezwungen
Und der gott nur gibt die richte
Wilder traum hinabgerungen
Wo ich mich in dir vernichte . .
Nun bestimmt die höhere sende
Wie ich mich in dir vollende.

What has been endured, allay!
Counterspirit now is bended,
And the god decrees the way,
Savage dream is downed and ended,
Where myself in you I slay . . .
Now a greater Fate has willed
How in you I be fulfilled.

WER SEINES REICHTUMS UNWERT IHN NICHT NUEZT
Muss weinen: nicht wer arm ist wer verlor . .
Du bist der gerte finder deren ruck
Verrät wo heilsam wasser steigen will
Und adern goldes in der tiefe ruhn.
Erschrick nicht staune nicht: "warum denn ich?"
Wirf nicht im trotz das wunderding beiseit
Weil du es nicht begreifst . . geniess und hilf
Solang der stab in deiner hand gehorcht.

He, who unworthy, does not use his wealth
Should weep: not who is poor or who has lost . . .
You are the finder of the rod whose jerk
Betrays where healing water wants to rise,
And veins of gold are slumbering in the depths.
Be not afraid, nor wonder: why just I?
Cast not the charm defiantly aside
Because you grasp it not . . . rejoice and help
As long as in your hand the wand obeys.

Du nennst es viel dass du zu eigen nimmst
Mein gut wie deins . . noch hast du nichts genannt!
Du wurdest mitbesitzer meiner stunden
Dein bitten ist bedenklich wie befehl.
Ich muss dein schirm sein wo du dich gefährdest
Den streich entgegennehmen der dir galt.
Ich bin für jeden deiner mängel bürge
Mir fallen alle deine lasten zu
Die als zu schwer du abwarfst—alle tränen
Die du sollst weinen und die du nicht weinst.

You say that it is much you took as yours
All I possess . . . but this says nothing yet!
You came to be the sharer of my hours,
Your pleading is precarious as command.
Your shelter I must be where you are perilled,
The blow encounter that was meant for you,
For every flaw you have, I am the voucher,
The burdens you discarded as too grave,
I must sustain them all—and all the tears
You ought to weep and that you never weep.

Wer je die flamme umschritt
Bleibe der flamme trabant!
Wie er auch wandert und kreist:
Wo noch ihr schein ihn erreicht
Irrt er zu weit nie vom ziel.
Nur wenn sein blick sie verlor
Eigener schimmer ihn trügt:
Fehlt ihm der mitte gesetz
Treibt er zerstiebend ins all.

Who once has circled the flame
Always shall follow the flame!
Far though he wander and turn:
Never too far from the goal
While he is reached by the light.
But when he loses its gleam,
Duped by a flash of his own:
Law of the center he leaves,
Shattered and driven through worlds.

Neuen adel den ihr suchet
Führt nicht her von schild und krone!
Aller stufen halter tragen
Gleich den feilen blick der sinne
Gleich den rohen blick der spähe . .
Stammlos wachsen im gewühle
Seltne sprossen eignen ranges
Und ihr kennt die mitgeburten
An der augen wahrer glut.

New nobility you wanted
Does not hail from crown or scutcheon!
Men of whatsoever level
Show their lust in venal glances,
Show their greeds in ribald glances . . .
Scions rare of rank intrinsic
Grow from masses, not from peerage,
And you will detect your kindred
By the light within their eyes.

GOTTES PFAD IST UNS GEWEITET
Gottes land ist uns bestimmt
Gottes krieg ist uns entzündet
Gottes kranz ist uns erkannt.
Gottes ruh in unsren herzen
Gottes kraft in unsrer brust
Gottes zorn auf unsren stirnen
Gottes brunst auf unsrem mund.
Gottes band hat uns umschlossen
Gottes blitz hat uns durchglüht
Gottes heil ist uns ergossen
Gottes glück ist uns erblüht.

PATH OF GOD TO US IS OPENED
Land of God for us decreed
War of God in us is kindled
Wreath of God on us bestowed.
Peace of God is in our pulses
Strength of God is in our breast
Wrath of God is on our foreheads
Flame of God is on our mouth.
Bond of God has now enwound us
Flash of God through us is glown
Bliss of God is poured around us
Joy of God for us is blown.

HYPERION

Ich kam zur heimat: solch gewog von blüten
Empfing mich nie . . ein pochen war im feld
In meinem hain von schlafenden gewalten,
Ich sah euch fluss und berg und gau im bann
Und brüder euch als künftige sonnen-erben:
In eurem scheuen auge ruht ein traum
Einst wird in euch zu blut der sehnsucht sinnen . . .
Mein leidend leben neigt dem schlummer zu
Doch gütig lohnt der Himmlischen verheissung
Dem frommen . . . der im Reich nie wandeln darf:
Ich werde heldengrab, ich werde scholle
Der heilige sprossen zur vollendung nahn:
MIT DIESEN KOMMT DAS ZWEITE ALTER, LIEBE
GEBAR DIE WELT, LIEBE GEBIERT SIE NEU.
Ich sprach den spruch, der zirkel ist gezogen . .
Eh mich das dunkel überholt entrückt
Mich hohe schau: bald geht mit leichten sohlen
Durch teure flur greifbar im glanz der Gott.

HYPERION

I journeyed home: such flood of blossoms never
Had welcomed me . . . a throbbing in the field
And in the grove there was of sleeping powers.
I saw the river, slope and shire enthralled,
And you, my brothers, sun-heirs of the future:
Your eyes, still chaste, are harboring a dream,
Once yearning thoughts in you, to blood shall alter . . .
My sorrow-stricken life to slumber leans,
But graciously does heaven's promise guerdon
The fervent . . . who may never pace the Realm.
I shall be earth, shall be the grave of heroes,
That sacred sons approach to be fulfilled.
WITH THEM THE SECOND AGE COMES, LOVE
    ENGENDERED
THE WORLD, AGAIN SHALL LOVE ENGENDER IT.
I spoke the spell, the circle has been woven . . .
Before the darkness falls, I shall be snatched
Aloft and know: through cherished fields shall wander
On weightless soles, aglow and real, the God.

GEBET

So hohes glück war keinem je erschienen
Dass er verharren dürft in seinem strahle,
Mit auf—und niedergang wird es bestehen . .
Ich muss mich neigen überm dunklen brunnen,
Die form aus seinen tiefen wieder suchen—
Anders und immer Du—und aufwärts holen . .
Die reichste feier will verjüngt sich sehen
Der flüchtigen von heut entnimmt sie dauer . .
So lass geschehn dass ich an jeder freude
Gemäss dem satz des lebens mich entfache!
Da uns die trübe droht wenn wir nicht strömen
Reisst oft sich unser geist aus seinen grenzen:
Vom glorreichen beginn an webt er träume
In reihen endlos bis in spätste zonen
Verfolgt er zug um zug verwegne spiele . .
Zujubelnd den erahnten morgenröten
Hängt er verzückt in unermessner schwebe.
Dann wieder schaut er aus wo sich ihm weise
Ein fester stern—dein stern—zu stetem preise
Und wo ein ruhen sei im allgekreise.

PRAYER

Such heights of joy by none were ever witnessed
That sojourn he was granted in their splendor,
In up and downward course they shall continue,
My heart is bowed above the sombre waters
Again to seek the form within the hollows—
Other and always You—and draw it upwards,
The richest fête is avid for renewal,
From fugitive Today it gleans endurance . . .
Then let it come to pass that I, affirming
The law of life, may glow with every rapture!
Since dulness threatens where there is no current
Our spirit often bursts beyond its borders:
From luminous beginnings, dreams it textures
To latest zones in series never ending,
It follows move for move the games of hazard,
It hails imagined dawns with exultation
And hovers spellbound in uncharted levels,
Then yearns again to find for its descrying
A steadfast star—your star—for praise undying,
And rest on planets ever lured and flying.

DER MENSCH UND DER DRUD

DER MENSCH

Das enge bachbett sperrt ein wasserfall—
Doch wer hängt das behaarte bein herab
Von dieses felsens träufelnd fettem moos?
Aus buschig krausem kopfe lugt ein horn . . .
So weit ich schon in waldgebirgen jagte
Traf ich doch seinesgleichen nie . . . Bleib still
Der weg ist dir verlegt, verbirg auch nichts!
Aus klarer welle schaut ein ziegenfuss.

DER DRUD

Nicht dich noch mich wird freun dass du mich fandst.

DER MENSCH

Ich wusste wol von dir verwandtem volk
Aus vorzeitlicher märe—nicht dass heut
So nutzlos hässlich ungetüm noch lebt.

DER DRUD

Wenn du den lezten meiner art vertriebst
Spähst du vergeblich aus nach edlem wild
Dir bleibt als beute nager und gewürm
Und wenn ins lezte dickicht du gebrochen
Vertrocknet bald dein nötigstes: der quell.

DER MENSCH

Du ein weit niedrer lehrst mich? Unser geist
Hat hyder riese drache greif erlegt
Den unfruchtbaren hochwald ausgerodet

MAN AND FAUN

MAN

A fall of water locks the narrow stream—
But who is there and hangs his shaggy leg
From lush and dripping mosses of this rock?
From bushy, curling pate protrudes a horn.
Though far on wooded mountains I have hunted,
His like I never yet have met . . . stay still,
The way is blocked to you, hide nothing here!
The limpid wave reveals a goaten foot.

THE FAUN

Your find will pleasure neither you nor me.

MAN

I knew indeed of creatures kin to you
From tales of long ago—not that today
Such useless, ugly monsters still survive.

THE FAUN

When you have driven off the last of us,
For noble quarry you will search in vain,
Your prey will be the gnawing beasts and worms,
And when you have invaded every thicket,
The drouth will take what most you need: the well.

MAN

You, one so base, would tutor me? Our mind
The hydra, giant, dragon, griffin slew,
And cleared the wilderness that bears no fruit.

Wo sümpfe standen wogt das ährenfeld
Im saftigen grün äst unser zahmes rind
Gehöfte städte blühn und helle gärten
Und forst ist noch genug für hirsch und reh—
Die schätze hoben wir von see und grund
Zum himmel rufen steine unsre siege . .
Was willst du überbleibsel grauser wildnis?
Das licht die ordnung folgen unsrer spur.

DER DRUD

Du bist nur mensch . . wo deine weisheit endet
Beginnt die unsre, du merkst erst den rand
Wo du gebüsst hast für den übertritt.
Wenn dein getreide reift dein vieh gedeiht
Die heiligen bäume öl und trauben geben
Wähnst du dies käme nur durch deine list.
Die erden die in dumpfer urnacht atmen
Verwesen nimmer, sind sie je gefügt
Zergehn sie wenn ein glied dem ring entfällt.
Zur rechten weile ist dein walten gut,
Nun eil zurück! du hast den Drud gesehn.
Dein schlimmstes weisst du selbst nicht: wenn dein
        sinn
Der vieles kann in wolken sich verfängt
Das band zerrissen hat mit tier und scholle—
Ekel und lust getrieb und einerlei
Und staub und strahl und sterben und entstehn
Nicht mehr im gang der dinge fassen kann.

DER MENSCH

Wer sagt dir so? dies sei der götter sorge.

Where marshes stood, the wheaten acre sways,
On sappy meadow, tame, our cattle browse,
Demesnes and cities bloom and shining gardens
And woods enough are left for stag and doe—
We lifted treasures from the sea and earth,
Our victories the stones proclaim to heaven,
What would you, relic of the awful jungle?
For order follows in our tracks and light.

THE FAUN

You are but man, and where your wisdom ends
Our own begins, you only see the brink
When you have suffered for the step beyond.
When ripe your grain has grown, your cattle thrive,
The sacred trees their oil and wine surrender,
You think this only comes through ruse of yours.
The earths that breathe in stolid nights primeval
Do not decay, if ever they were joined
They sunder when a link escapes the ring.
Your rule is right for your appointed time.
Now hasten back! You have beheld the faun.
The worst, you do not know, is that your mind
Which can do much, in clouds may be enmeshed,
May rend apart the bond with clod and creature—
Loathing and lust, monotony and flux,
And dust and light and death and being born,
No more will grasp within the course of things.

MAN

Who tells you so? For this the gods be sponsors.

DER DRUD

Wir reden nie von ihnen, doch ihr toren
Meint dass sie selbst euch helfen. Unvermittelt
Sind sie euch nie genaht. Du wirst du stirbst—
Wess wahr geschöpf du bist erfährst du nie.

DER MENSCH

Bald ist kein raum mehr für dein zuchtlos spiel.

DER DRUD

Bald rufst du drinnen den du draussen schmähst.

DER MENSCH

Du giftiger unhold mit dem schiefen mund
Trotz deiner missgestalt bist du der unsren
Zu nah, sonst träfe jezt dich mein geschoss . .

DER DRUD

Das tier kennt nicht die sham der mensch nicht dank.
Mit allen künsten lernt ihr nie was euch
Am meisten frommt . . wir aber dienen still.
So hör nur dies: uns tilgend tilgt ihr euch.
Wo unsre zotte streift nur da kommt milch
Wo unser huf nicht hintritt wächst kein halm.
Wär nur dein geist am werk gewesen: längst
Wär euer schlag zerstört und all sein tun
Wär euer holz verdorrt und saatfeld brach . .
Nur durch den zauber bleibt das leben wach.

THE FAUN

We never speak of them, but in your folly
You think they help you; without go-betweens
They never came to you: you dawn, you die—
Whose thing you are in truth, you never learn.

MAN

Soon you will have no space for shameless sport.

THE FAUN

Soon whom you spurn without, you call within.

MAN

You poisonous monster with the crooked mouth,
Despite your twisted shape, you are too kindred
To ours, or else my dart would strike you now.

THE FAUN

The beast is void of shame, the man of thanks.
With all contrivances you never learn
What most you need . . . but we in silence serve.
This only: slaying us, you slay yourselves.
Where we have trailed our shag, there spurts the milk,
Where we withheld our hooves, there grows no grass.
Your mind alone at work—and long ago
Your kind had been destroyed and all it does.
Your field would lie unsown and dry your brake . . .
Only by magic, Life is kept awake.

Tauch hinab in den strom
Den das weidicht umrauscht
Den der mond überblinkt!
Was dich bestimmt hat bei tag
Alle hüllen wirf ab
Aller trug wird verspült!
Schauernd steigst du herauf
Zwischen mir und der nacht . .
Was die hand dich nun heischt
Was dem mund sich entringt
Probt was in wahrheit du giltst.

Be immersed in the stream
That the willows ensurge,
That the moon overgleams!
What has impelled you by day,
All that covers you, doff,
All of sham flows afar.
Trembling upward you rise
Between me and the night . . .
What the hand now commands,
What the mouth stirs to word,
Proves what is really your worth.

Du kennst die traumeswelt: du wirst verstehen,
Mit tages tat werd ich dich nie bezwingen
Mit tages rat wirst du mich nie erringen
Der dichte wind der träume muss erst wehen

Sie wandeln, färben jedes ding im rund
Dass wir es in der echten form erkennen
Dass wir es mit dem wahren namen nennen,
Doch was ertönen macht das ist dein mund.

You see the world of dreams, and so you know
With deed of day you cannot be compelled,
With plans of day I never shall be held,
The heavy winds of dream have first to blow.

They change, they color everything around,
That in its proper form we may behold it,
That with its real name we may enfold it,
But yours the mouth that makes it all resound.

DER TAENZER

Im garten wiegt der kinder ringelreihn
In weiche luft des abends dringt ihr sang
Sie ziehn in paaren schwingen sich im kreise
Und hüpfen nach des gleichen liedes weise
Wie sie sich froh die kleinen hände leihn!
Doch Einer gibt den takt an und den gang.

Wie leicht sein fuss sich dreht und schnellt und säumt
Wie beugt die hüfte sich gewandt und sacht!
Im dunkel zittert seines haares schimmer
Er ist der leuchtstern mitten im geflimmer
Er ist die ganze jugend wie sie träumt
Er ist die ganze jugend wie sie lacht.

THE DANCER

Through gardens rocks the children's roundelay,
Their song the gentle air of evening grooves,
In pairs they sally, dance in circles swinging,
And hop in rhythm to the selfsame singing,
How glad, each little hand in hand, they sway!
But One there is who marks the beats and moves.

How soft and lithe his hip in bending seems,
With turn and stop his nimble foot beguiles!
His hair in darkness sheds a trembling shimmer,
He is the lodestar in the midst of glimmer,
He is the whole of youth with all its dreams,
He is the whole of youth with all its smiles.

Horch was die dumpfe erde spricht:
Du frei wie vogel oder fisch—
Worin du hängst, das weisst du nicht.

Vielleicht entdeckt ein spätrer mund:
Du sassest mit an unsrem tisch
Du zehrtest mit von unsrem pfund.

Dir kam ein schön und neu gesicht
Doch zeit ward alt, heut lebt kein mann
Ob er je kommt das weisst du nicht

Der dies gesicht noch sehen kann.

Hear stolid earth that speaks below:
You, free as fish and fowls of air—
Wherein you cling, you do not know.

A later mouth may once reveal:
You spended with us of our share,
You tasted with us of our meal.

You saw a vision wax and glow,
But Time grew old—none lives today,
If one will come, you do not know,

Who still could bid this vision stay.

SEELIED

Wenn an der kimm in sachtem fall
Eintaucht der feurig rote ball:
Dann halt ich auf der düne rast
Ob sich mir zeigt ein lieber gast.

Zu dieser stund ists öd daheim,
Die blume welkt im salzigen feim.
Im lezten haus beim fremden weib
Tritt nie wer unter zum verbleib.

Mit gliedern blank mit augen klar
Kommt nun ein kind mit goldnem haar,
Es tanzt und singt auf seiner bahn
Und schwindet hinterm grossen kahn.

Ich schau ihm vor, ich schau ihm nach
Wenn es auch niemals mit mir sprach
Und ich ihm nie ein wort gewusst:
Sein kurzer anblick bringt mir lust.

SEASONG

When on the verge with gentle fall
Down dips the fire-reddened ball,
Then on the dunes I pause to rest
That I may see a cherished guest.

This time of day is dull at home,
The flower wilts in salty foam,
And in a house so far away
With alien woman, none will stay.

With naked limbs, with cloudless eye
A goldhaired child now passes by,
It sings and dances as it nears,
Behind the boat it disappears.

I watch it come, I watch it go,
Though never words for it I know,
And never speech for me it had,
The brief beholding makes me glad.

Mein herd ist gut, mein dach ist dicht,
Doch eine freude wohnt dort nicht.
Die netze hab ich all geflickt
Und küch und kammer sind beschickt.

So sitz ich, wart ich auf dem strand
Die schläfe pocht in meiner hand:
Was hat mein ganzer tag gefrommt
Wenn heut das blonde kind nicht kommt.

My hearth is good, my roof is tight,
But bare it is of all delight.
The rents in every net I sewed,
And room and kitchen are bestowed.

So then I sit and wait astrand,
My temple pulses in my hand:
What use the day from dawn to dawn
If now the blondhaired child is gone!

DAS WORT

Wunder von ferne oder traum
Bracht ich an meines landes saum

Und harrte bis die graue norn
Den namen fand in ihrem born—

Drauf konnt ichs greifen dicht und stark
Nun blüht und glänzt es durch die mark . . .

Einst langt ich an nach guter fahrt
Mit einem kleinod reich und zart

Sie suchte lang und gab mir kund:
'So schläft hier nichts auf tiefem grund'

Worauf es meiner hand entrann
Und nie mein land den schatz gewann . . .

So lernt ich traurig den verzicht:
Kein ding sei wo das wort gebricht.

THE WORD

Wonder of dream and distant land
I carried to my country's strand

And waited till the twilit norn
Had found the name within her bourn—

Then I could grasp it near and strong
It blooms and shines now through the throng . . .

Once I returned from happy sail,
I had a jewel rich and frail,

She sought for long and tiding told:
'No like of this these depths enfold.'

And straight it vanished from my hand,
The treasure never graced my land . . .

I learned then sadly to desist:
Where words default, no things exist.

DAS LICHT

Wir sind in trauer wenn, uns minder günstig
Du dich zu andren, mehr beglückten, drehst
Wenn unser geist, nach anbetungen brünstig,
An abenden in deinem abglanz wes't.

Wir wären töricht, wollten wir dich hassen
Wenn oft dein strahl verderbendrohend sticht
Wir wären kinder, wollten wir dich fassen—
Da du für alle leuchtest, süsses Licht!

THE LIGHT

We are in grief, when less on us bestowing
Your grace, you turn to others gladdened more,
When eventides in your reflected glowing
Our spirit lingers, yearning to adore.

We should be fools to let our hatred grasp you,
Though often with your blaze you threaten blight,
We should be children if we tried to clasp you—
Because you shine for one and all: Sweet Light!

In stillste ruh
Besonnenen tags
Bricht jäh ein blick
Der unerahnten schrecks
Die sichre seele stört

So wie auf höhn
Der feste stamm
Stolz reglos ragt
Und dann noch spät ein sturm
Ihn bis zum boden beugt:

So wie das meer
Mit gellem laut
Mit wildem prall
Noch einmal in die lang
Verlassne muschel stösst.

Through deepest rest
Of ordered day
A glance has flashed,
That troubles with a fear
Undreamed the tranquil soul.

Just as on heights
The solid stem
Proud, moveless looms,
And late a tempest bends
It downward to the ground:

Just as the tide
With strident sound,
With savage lunge,
Once more into the long
Abandoned sea-shell thrusts.

Du schlank und rein wie eine flamme
Du wie der morgen zart und licht
Du blühend reis vom edlen stamme
Du wie ein quell geheim und schlicht

Begleitest mich auf sonnigen matten
Umschauerst mich im abendrauch
Erleuchtest meinen weg im schatten
Du kühler wind du heisser hauch

Du bist mein wunsch und mein gedanke
Ich atme dich mit jeder luft
Ich schlürfe dich mit jedem tranke
Ich küsse dich mit jedem duft

Du blühend reis vom edlen stamme
Du wie ein quell geheim und schlicht
Du schlank und rein wie eine flamme
Du wie der morgen zart und licht.

You flawless as a flame and slender,
You flower sprung from Crown and Spear,
You as the morning, light and tender,
You secret as a spring and clear,

Companion me in sunny meadows,
Entremble me in evening haze,
You shine upon my path through shadows,
You cool of wind, you breath of blaze.

You are my dreaming and my waking,
The air I breathe with you is pent,
In every draught you are my slaking,
And you I kiss in every scent.

You as the morning, light and tender,
You flower sprung from Crown and Spear,
You flawless as a flame and slender,
You secret as a spring and clear.

DIE GEDICHTE

HYMNEN · PILGERFAHRTEN · ALGABAL

DIE BUECHER DER HIRTEN – UND PREISGEDICHTE

DAS JAHR DER SEELE

DER TEPPICH DES LEBENS

THE POEMS

HYMNS · PILGRIMAGES · ALGABAL

THE BOOKS OF ECLOGUES AND EULOGIES

THE YEAR OF THE SOUL

THE TAPESTRY OF LIFE

DIE GEDICHTE

THE POEMS

THE SEVENTH RING

DIE GEDICHTE

DER STERN DES BUNDES

DAS NEUE REICH

THE POEMS

METHOD AND PURPOSE OF THE TRANSLATION

THE POEMS IN THIS BOOK, taken from the seven volumes that constitute George's main work, were selected with a view to affording insight into the thought and art of the poet. The goal of the translation was to imitate the form as well as to give the content of the poems. This meant more than a superficial following of the rhythms of the text. The inner rhythm of the original had to be traced and cast into adequate English form. Every line was examined to find where the emphasis lay in thought and in rhythm. The same was done with each stanza and finally with the entire poem, for the distribution of weight in the parts and in the whole is of the utmost significance and gives poems the special tone and force that draw the hearer into their spell. It is even important to distribute the long and short syllables as in the original. Every verse in poetry has its own deliberately chosen caesura which either increases the tension or has a retarding effect. By observing this caesura, a change in thought, imagery or tone can be indicated through the movement of the verse. The line of the original was maintained as a whole as far as possible. Never was a verse from one stanza shifted to another and the stanzas themselves were always kept intact.

Two fundamental differences between English and German had to be dealt with: adjective versus verb and the handling of relative clauses. In German it is usual to construct a sentence so that the main clause frames many subordinate clauses. Since the English structure is much more loosely knit, a way had to be found not to blur the relative values of main and subordinate clauses. Descriptive richness in German is given by the adjective, by whole processions of adjectives and by compound adjectives. In English this makes for bombast rather than beauty. Whenever it was possible, the color of the adjective was shifted to the verb and verbs were actually substituted for adjectives. The composite adjective was rendered by a phrase, though occasionally a particularly striking combination was verbally translated to convey the word-creative power of the poet. For too great a fear of foreign locutions may produce the undesirable extreme of reducing the mass and splendor of the original in favor of the customary and the inoffensive.

The rhyme schemes of all rhymed poems were closely observed and in almost all cases internal rhyme and assonance were reproduced. Since English has many more monosyllabic words than German and fewer rhyme possibilities, it was not always feasible to retain the frequent alternations between masculine and feminine endings in the rhymed poems. But it was found that in English, certain endings of monosyllables, particularly the endings m and r, produced the effect a second weightless syllable had in German. In the unrhymed poems, masculine and feminine endings were observed in almost every case, for without this, the effect would not have approximated the original. Both in the rhymed and unrhymed poems the many alliterations were followed. Indeed it frequently occurred that alliteration was desirable in English to make a line more solid, and that only then it was discovered that the German text had approaches to alliteration which had been overlooked, but the force of which had carried over in feeling where it had evaded thought. Altogether many subtleties of the original that are not apparent even after intensive readings, came to the fore in translating. The effect achieved by the contrast between light and dark vowels or by a procession of dark or light vowel sounds was maintained. The use of consonants was imitated: sibilant or liquid or massed consonants, since this is one of the direct avenues to the imagination of the hearer.

The tone level on which a poet begins and ends a verse, a stanza or a whole poem, is characteristic of the style. Just as one can attribute paintings of unknown origin to certain artists on the basis of the brush strokes, one very important criterion for the attribution of a poem is the tone of the beginning, the level on which it is sustained and the rise or drop or gradual dying out at the end. It is crucial to the tone whether a line consists of long or short words or of a special blend of long and short words, and this tone must carry over to the inner ear. The poems of George are intended to be recited in such a way that, as in the classical and Romance languages, the rhythm, not the content, is emphasized. In such a form of recitation the pause for breath is most important and the way in which the breath is taken depends upon the combination of long and short words.

The purpose of this translation is to acquaint the English speaking reader with a world of poetry and thought that is as significant for cultural development as that of Goethe and Nietzsche. Beyond this, the translation has the value of a commentary even for those who are familiar with the language of the original. George coined a language of his own which presents extraordinary difficulties in vocabulary and construction, apart from the obscurities in meaning, which cannot be solved with the usual apparatus for research. Up to now there is no comprehensive commentary on his work. The translators were in a position to use unpublished material, such as notes on conversations with Stefan George, in which the poet himself discussed every poem of his works with the author of the introduction who was then beginning his task of commenting. The language used in translation must be intelligible in word and structure. This criterion sometimes made it necessary to elucidate the original, not by additions or omissions, but by a choice of such words from the wealth of English words deriving from the Latin and the Anglo-Saxon, as would serve to clarify the meaning. Nowhere, however, have art values been violated by the intrusion of purely rational analysis, for the chief concern of the translators was to give an English equivalent of the original in its magic.

Carol North Valhope   *Ernst Morwitz*